v v v

Nature
Knows
The
Way

v v v

Foreword

Poets are often obsessed with nature & the cycles of the seasons, because nature anchors us to reality. The modern world is so full of computers, social media, complicated relationships, and a drive to get things done that it's easy to lose our connection to the world we live in. Inspiration is easy to find when you just sit and feel the sun on your skin, listen to the birds, feel the dry wind blowing in distant scents.

Nature understands that all things change -it doesn't hold on, but also doesn't entirely follow a schedule. Neither does life - but when we focus on our observations and take time to respond deliberately lets us make connections between simple nature & our more complicated human lives.

Walk with us on this journey, let the scenes we write about take you there. Let our experience inform and inspire your experience.

Table of Contents

[Jordón Shinn]

Elegy for a Cellist

I will remember
the scent of your coiled hair
as we held each other there
on the floorboards
under the orange porch light —

as you stood on my toes
and I breathed so gently
through my nose
above the sacred curve
of your exposed collar bone.

Warm earth, sun soil,
sweet, rich, exfoliating —
as if you were born among the raspberry
bushes and wild crocus weeds.
How you bloomed beside the woodpile
on tufted Bermuda grass

in the pasture's summer shadows,
where we lay breathing,
hushed and heavily —
just us
and the fireflies
and the black cows lowing.

I will remember
your voice, sung
through the bell-shaped wood box —
white bow hairs flung
on sheep gut strings.

How the cello bellowed
a Popper étude,
ebbing like lake water
in the palm of your body.

How you shook the whole world —
the green and pink painted room,
the chair, the cello,
your brown twisting bangs
swinging.

Jordón Shinn is a Bangkok-based creative writer from Brooklyn.
A longtime expat in Asia, his poetry collections include 'Forest
Talk' and 'Echoes from the West Side.' Follow @
jordonious.worpdress.com Allpoetry.com/Papyrus

[Robert E. Ray]

thresholds

Be not simply good——be good for something.
——Henry David Thoreau

go to the front window, look out, look up.
see the chaff, the yellow ribbon, the nest
the little pink heads & tipped bills, the white grub
from the girl cardinal, her reddish crest
up against the stiff wind, the bright red boy
in the holly—*wheat, wheat, wheat, tew, tew, tew.*
never disturb the nest. never destroy
what's not yours. the bird is not there for you.

we share the sun, the air, the patched tin roof.
the bird makes its safe place and you make yours.
open the front door, step out. hear the hoofs
on the road, crows in the oaks, see the wires
of sparrows, wind in the corn—the carriage pass.
wave. shoo the new birds away from the glass.

———————

R.E. Ray is a retired public servant. His poetry has been published by Rattle, Beyond Words International Literary Magazine, Wild Roof Journal, The Ekphrastic Review and in four poetry anthologies. Allpoetry.com/R.E._Ray

Old Furniture

inside the onion tough leathery skin
caught underneath
layers of primrose carpets
pink dipped
finding the ultimate union with
myself

age will breathe
its last breath
slowly bringing air
into lungs deeply
falling from the distant world
because inside here everything
is perfect
because it's empty
because it's perfect
with emptiness

silver coverings
wrapped in a cocoon
with no preconceptions.
swallowing surroundings immediately
flickering faces
dark with separation
evenly divided
by thin silky shadows

a world stuffed into a case.
filled with truth
all things rendered useless
nourished only by floating facts
accumulated dusted off
and recollected
in a space ruled by inertia
where all things
remains the same
untouched unmoved

and all objects remain
unaltered hidden closets
watching clockwork
run blindly from a cross
decomposed Inside
button bodice gloves
skull bone shuffling substances
mixing with the past

lost In a dream,
drilling into the marrow
of existence
bones becoming
floating picture books
of blank pages
walking up and down
wandering
whispering pines

searching for a street sign
called "meek mercy"

I know the stained-glass window
inside me
the old foyer
three flights of stairs
lined with rocking chairs
the house with its parquet floors
furniture covered and
uninhabited

Poet, podcast host and author who has been writing poetry for 50
years in the modern genre.

Born in Miami, Florida, currently residing in Germany

Poetry podcast host and co-host of Delving in a Moment
Allpoetry.com/Chinaski

[Brian Thomas Duffield]

Dying breath

Distain the dark, await the dawn's first light
when blackened clouds are dressed by gilts extreme.
Rain, rain with russet leaves in broken flight.

Follow the scent of ripened apple blight
as autumn's breath exhales a foggy steam.
Distain the dark, await the dawn's first light.

Warm your hands as brittle branches ignite
and purple veins in wiry knots redeem.
Rain, rain with russet leaves in broken flight.

Listen when wailing wind the shards delight
as oboes play a dirgeful tragic theme.
Distain the dark, await the dawn's first light.

A winter tree with swathes of speckled blight
in swirling gold the fitful fragments stream.
Rain, rain with russet leaves in broken flight.

You lie in limbo, blindly seeking sight
as cloudy mists exhale o'er moors agleam.
Distain the dark, await the dawn's first light.
Rain, rain with russet leaves in broken flight.

Brian Thomas Duffield is originally from Newcastle upon Tyne but now lives in Lancaster in the United Kingdom. He retired from a lifetime teaching English and now spends his time writing poetry. Allpoetry.com/Brian_T_Duffield

[Liz Masters]

Drained

Door closed,
twisted lock,
alone.

Behind the curtain,
water falls; burns
like the acid
rising in my throat,
wanting out.

Music pounds;
drowns the sound
of my exhale.

I envy the water
that pools around my feet,
swirls toward the drain
and is swallowed down,
gone.

I step out;
one foot,
then the next,
against the hard, damp floor

to face
what's behind fogged glass,
staring back,
with wet hair, wild,
in an old shirt with holes;

worthy, a whisper,
while the mirror screams no.

Liz currently lives in Memphis, TN but feels most at home up near the Great Lakes. She wears many hats, teacher and adventurer among her favorites, and writing is how she first discovered her voice. Allpoetry.com/Liz_Masters

[Robert Poleski]

Beauty

where shall you seek beauty and
how shall you find her
unless- she herself be your way and guide-
and how shall you speak of her except
she be the weaver of your speech

it's not the image you perceive
nor the song you can hear
you behold her through your closed eyes
and the song heard
though your ears are shut

her beauty is of soft whisper
speaking to my spirit
her voice yields to our silences
like a faint light
the light that quivers in the fear of shadow

she walks among us
shakes the earth beneath and the sky above
comes with the spring leaping upon the hills
in the summer dancing with the autumn leaves
once we saw a drift of snow in her hair-

beauty is not a mouth thirsting nor an empty hand stretched forth
but rather the heart enchanted
it is not the sap within the furrowed bark

nor a wing attached to a claw
but rather a garden forever in bloom
and a flock of angels forever in flight

beauty is a poem in every flower
and a sonnet in every tree
the flowers bespeckled with dew
in the thin dawn's light
the bluebells carpet of the woodland floor
colored leaves in the autumnal forest
brown skinned arms waving in woodland winds
and the tree fungus and the spotted frog

beauty is brief and mighty like the white thunderbolt
stony trails of a jagged beauty rise
like stretch marks streaking sand-hips
she's in the touch of your hand
an amazement of the baby
when they first meet a dog or
see a leaf move in the wind

beauty is in the trees-
the dancing ladies
choreographed by the wind
as they stretch upwards and outwards toward the light
drinking in rays as pure as the rain--
a stand of pines- a bone-thin phalanx
bending- listen to
the autumn wind as it mutters
flanking the roadside

I stretch my arms up too
fingers spread toward the sun
and slowly
begin to dance
hear the soft song of the wind
as soothing as the sweetest of lullabies
for there are daisies that grow tall and pure upon our earth
reaching upwards in sunshine
blessed by rain

harvest the beauty where it grows
from the blackest night to the whitest light of day
in the clouds which sail above
creating new art by the moment
in that freely given casual smile
that adventurous light spark in your eye
a melody beyond the range of ears
but heard inside your mind
beauty hidden
among the tangle of bush and trees
is free
free for all to enjoy
free enough to rescue us all

———————————

I am biased. What I see and write about is my inner world, an intimate universe, trying to find my place in the real world, change it if I can to fit my picture of reality, but mostly to adapt to it. Allpoetry.com/Robert_Poleski

[S. Libellule]

Nature Knows the Way

Life is an unmarked trail
an untrimmed sail
yet even still in the squall
nature knows the way

Which way to then lead
each waterspout and bent reed
points in the right direction
an outer path deep within

For the wisdom of the trees
is shared upon the breeze
written on bone runes
written in lone poetry

About the solace of breath
in a denouement of death
when the script is flipped
the chorus now mute

While I savor the verdant hush
step into the bramble bush
trade in all these brass rings
for more arboreal things

Originally from New England, Libellule currently lives outside of Birmingham, Alabama. Poetic influences include Mary Oliver, Billy Collins and ee cummings. Allpoetry.com/Little_Dragonfly

[David E. Navarro]
Just Walk

I looked for life on a dusty trail
kicked a rock along for miles and
saw a shooting star;

gazed up into the sky for life
watched red-tailed hawks soar and
imagined shapes in the clouds;

panned for life wading in the river
felt the current pull my feet and
heard brown trout leap in the air;

waited on my porch rocker for life
chatted with some neighbors and
felt love and good cheer.

I was looking for myself in life...
and found that I was there
living large—and full and free.

It's not in the fiery sun, pale moon,
hurling planets, or flickering stars;
not in vast continents, deep seas,
or massive mountain ranges;

it's in a simple well-worn rock—
just walk and look and see.

David E Navarro is an author, poet-philosopher, essayist and editor in Tucson AZ. Internet search 'David E. Navarro poet' for links to his books and work. Visit www.de-navarro.com for full bio/info. Allpoetry.com/D.E._Navarro

[David I Mayerhoff]

Variation and Renewal

The moon emerges over the lake
and a shadow lurks in the background
it advances to attack mode
as creatures of the night
spring from crypts, fangs and teeth
hunting the daytime wildlife
who now recede to their cubbyholes

the sense of the unique
pervades the dark
as we plug into forms of life
not present in sunlight

the flying birds morph into predatory commandos
when just last minute
they were saying hello
begging for crumbs

always the novel
the moon fosters new beginnings
as we reflect on
the daring novelties of nature

the howl becomes a gasp
the dark of night a terror soup

with the brain flashing many images
all outdo the last one in fear elicited

no time for cobwebs
as we dust off the tarantulas
to meet the next level of chilled nightmare
checking our pulse for sinus rhythm
and our watch for time to daybreak

David I Mayerhoff is a literary writer, poet, scientific author and Clinical Professor of Psychiatry. He grew up on Long Island and now resides in New Jersey. Allpoetry.com/David_Mayerhoff

[Andrew Stull]

dream home & my death

there is a beach
waiting on me.

a house with a wraparound porch
and a green wooden swing
where I'll drink coffee with the sunrise
and chamomile tea while the werewolves
howl at the moon.

an office where I'll write poetry,
novels, musings, and affirmations
on sticky notes.

a bathroom with a fat bellied tub
and a window that overlooks my garden
where jalapenos grow in August
and pumpkins come alive in October.

I'll live in my dream home
doing the things I love.

the peppers and chicken will roast
in my kitchen oven
while the pasta boils
and I sit at my
kitchen island counter
while I try to figure out
how a new story
ends.

my bedroom will have two ceiling
fans and black curtains to keep
out the sun.
my bed will be made of
marshmallows and my
sheets silk.
there's a painting hanging
near my nightstand;
I've been experimenting
with oils and this robin
turned out
neat.

my hair will grow gray,
my teeth will fall out,
and then
I
will
die.

in my dream home,
I
will
die.

Andrew is a nurse's aid from Clarksburg, West Virginia. He uses
poetry to cope with bipolar disorder. His favorite song is Read
My Mind by The Killers. His favorite meal is spaghetti and
meatballs. Allpoetry.com/Andrew_Stull

[James A. Hartley]

Eve

Where the waterfall breaks
and the streams swarm with shoals;

where the beasts shuffle on the banks
and birds stream across the first morning sky
my eyes
are only on you -

your shapes in the leaves as you yawn and stretch
your mesmerising line
and dark and darker depths:

there is nothing else in the world for me
though all is new and fresh and clear:

we lock eyes.

In your beauty I live and die;
yours another nature, apart.

You draw me like water over rocks
fast, breaking
to the fall.

———————————

J.A. Hartley lives in Madrid with his wife (to whom Eve is
dedicated) and his two children, Carmen Elise and Matthew
Benjamin. He likes a pint. Allpoetry.com/J._A._Hartley

[Marta Green]

Shadows of Pachelbel's Cannon

heavenly musical notes float in the air
a symphony sending lush sounds
delicate segments a great thrill
making delighted patrons gasp

a Harp solo, sounds of peace and serenity
like a delicate bird of Paradise
soft vibrations linger
graceful hands pluck bass on the strings

polished Cellos and a Violins bowing delicately
magical duet together
like tip toeing up a staircase
slow scales rise up, following each other round by round

lost in beauty with images of white waterfalls
clear blue seas lap at the shore
lounging in the brilliant yellow sun
bringing an echo to the end

Marta Green is an avid poetry and short story writer. Her passions are also family, friends, art and animals. She currently lives in Texas. Allpoetry.com/Marta_Green

[Annette Jane Gagliardi]

All's Black, Maroon & Navy

Once you had to die to be
laid in black, yet come on back
to the sack of darkness, lead
the way for a ray of smooth —
closely woven weave
which leaves no room for light,
to squeeze in.

Velvet softness sluffs
as it slides over my body,
tender on my skin.
It's not a sin to think darker
colors in black, maroon, navy
slim and serve to sexify.

Inky intensity of dusky
hues, betray pastel tones
and use deeply stamped shade
to cast tranquil repose that flows
moonless and starless into
tenebrous pores.

I am warmed and soothed
without illumination —
cozy in the fabric. Feel
the fabulousness of shade,

in its silky, sodden and
sultry home.

———————————

Annette Gagliardi is a Minnesota author and poet. She shares her
love of language within the League of Minnesota Poets and in the
general public. See her website at: https://annette-gagliardi.com
Allpoetry.com/Annette45

[David Scott Storm]

Climbing Trees

Grab a branch with a hand or knee,
And up you go into the tallest tree,
There among the leaves and breeze.
On sturdy limb, or branch, bent leaf,
Higher still, each step you take,
hand and foot, inch by inch,
the tree, tips...-sways and quakes.
The limbs begin to thin and shake,
Yes! The strength of sturdy branch!
Gives you courage, so up you stretch.!
Up, Up! the bluest sky is near..
And there,- so far below
bikers, walkers, squirrels, pets, cars
passing by, to and fro.
A king so high up in his tower,
can't have command,
his subjects power.
For up among that tallest tree,
is I the king who climbed a tree.

———————————

Robert Thomas Hall, grew up in big city, Detroit MI ..-but grew deeper roots along Michigan's beautiful scenic Upper Peninsula's Lake Superior shorelines. Allpoetry.com/RobertThomasHall

[David I Mayerhoff]

Struggles of Forward Progress

the race to the finish line
like the heart racing to a flat-line end
or to life-giving sinus rhythm

the pounding of flesh and sweat
on the road to discovery
to extricate the ember of the novel
and deliver it like a halfback
through the world's pile-on tackle

the colors of discovery
drive the engines of despair
to seek beyond the limits
the next internet without the virus

if only I could see through the dense fog
between the crevices of building blocks
at the kernel waiting to be dug out

for all the world to touch, feel, benefit
and know
that future is now

David I Mayerhoff is a literary and poetic writer, established
scientific author, and Clinical Professor of Psychiatry. He grew up
on Long Island and now resides in New Jersey.
Allpoetry.com/David_Mayerhoff

[David E. Navarro]

Yonder Pond

At yonder pond I ponder on
the frog's engaging stare
as flies go round and round and then
a fish jumps in the air.

Profuse the sweat runs down my face
under this sopping sky
and Sol seethes on throughout the day
for man and dragonfly.

To energize all life on Earth
precisely every day
the cosmic cycle ticking on...
endless minutiae.

Frogs and flies and fish abound
and I appreciate
at yonder pond I ponder on
until it's very late.

———————————

David E Navarro is an author, poet-philosopher, essayist and editor in Tucson AZ. Internet search 'David E. Navarro poet' for links to his books and work. Visit www.de-navarro.com for full bio/info. Allpoetry.com/D.E._Navarro

[James Hartley]
A Visit To Tita Carmen

She's one hundred and three
and I'm her time machine
showing her pictures on the strange machine
I keep in my pocket which she sees
and says, 'Oh! That's me!'

What do I say when she asks where the dead are?
Her sister? All her friends?
(I say 'they're at home' and she nods, satisfied).
I hold her hand which trembles,
which once knitted sleeves
she held a tape to, needles in her pursed lips,
looking at me as my grandmother cooed
and said, 'It fits!'

Once she was a girl, like this tree she planted
was a seed. Her roots are the deepest of the family
knitted to the foundations of our old house
built as she looked on, holding her mother's hand,
bound to a time that's slipped away
its music now passé,
its fashions in yellowing magazines,
its hopes and dreams in me somewhere,
like her.
Like family. Like the sea
we all once crawled from.

The elm towers beside me
and I water these plants she first showed me
when I was young, on holiday from the city.
She was and is my great aunty -
a lay-nun, a traveller, a business woman,
sister to my grandmother who was once young
and sang like a sparrow in the dripping dawn.
Her song lives on in the old woman's dream
I interrupt with shouted questions and my phone screen.

With her I am a girl again. Outside,
wife and mum. Inside, I'm old -
hot flushes, white streams in my hair -
to my husband I am beautiful, he says.
'How was your aunty?'
Deaf. Quiet.
Different. The same.
I look up:
the rain has stopped
and my children come running.

James Alexander Luke Hartley was born near Everton, England,
on a rainy Thursday 10th May, 1973. He now lives near Madrid,
Spain, with his wife Ana and his two kids, Seets and Matso
Nagasaki. Allpoetry.com/J._A._Hartley

[Stewart Brennan]

Under the Ruins

In the quiet moments of passing moon,
when the owl glides through obsidian air,
not a heartbeat is heard
but the thump is felt
as talons grasp prey on the dunes.

Those left behind are spattered in mourning,
sand, a silver glow smothered by shadows,
many heartbeats are heard
and their thumping's felt
by empathic witnesses under the ruins.

_____

Stewart Brennan is a poet on AP who enjoys writing about nature, the human condition, economics and politics. He's the author of three revealing books called, "The Activist Poet" (Vol 1, 2 & 3) Allpoetry.com/Minstral

[Mr. Ian Sane]

no burden

I.

carry no burden heavier than water
which can be returned to the sea
wish for no bounty greater
than simple divinity
of spirits which bind the soul
beyond the sphere, the world whole

II.

sink not into despair, rise, rise
to the blue sky, the yellow sun
brightly it burns, the retina, the skin
when lost think of the light of life
breath an intelligible
gift

---

guilty was born by a sailor and a gypsy in New Orleans...or in the
back seat of a cab in Central Park...either way he grew up to be
fine young man who cheated, lied and seduced his way into
various mi Allpoetry.com/Guilty

[Marius Alexandru]

Thankful

Today I am so glad,
I'm thankful for mom and dad,
for their patience, love, and care,
for my little teddy bear,
my sister, my brother,
grandpa, grandmother,
friends from the old school,
Zeus, my dog... he's cool!
God knows that it's true,
I'm thankful for all of you.

Marius Alexandru, from Chicago, is a published author of the books Ring of Fire Poems, Reflection of Thoughts, and many other poems in Poetry Anthologies in both English and Romanian languages. Allpoetry.com/Marius_Alexandru

[Arthur Goikhman]

Rhymosaurus

they call me Rhymosaurus
I freestyle and I rap
I don't need a thesaurus
to make you clap, clap, clap

love wearing my old headphones
and rapping to my beat
I feel it in my bones, bones
and that is pretty neat

A. Gee has been playing with words since he was little, and has finally been talked into sharing. His work can be described as Dr. Seuss meets Chaucer. Halfway at least!

Allpoetry.com/Agee

[Sandy L Galacio]

Tranquility & Peril - a Binary

TRANQUILITY

The ship lifts, pauses plunges
spray whips an empty deck
above the bulging main topsail floats
a pale blue translucent bubble
hanging full and by
fading stars strung like pearls
weave across an azure sky

A crescent of sun breaks from the ocean
first glow of day strikes the main tops
pauses brief to gather hold
liquid gold slivers down the shrouds
spreads across the dampened deck
lights the curls of nearby rollers
brightens the edges of sailcloth clouds

Seamen chant a salty shanty
bare footsteps beat an old tattoo
men haul rope against wind and rudder
urge the ship to change the tack
soon she gathers traction, hard to starboard
bone in her teeth, cream under her counter
another league toward home

PERIL

A mist ghosts by in layered veils
the sea shines through the gloom
flat and unruffled like pewter plate
portending a sudden doom
unlike a sea with a steady roll
set surfing before a breeze
stillness offered inefficient flow
to mark a barky's speed
with little wind to fill her sails
our minds were ill at ease

The pirate Captain hid his ship
behind the misty haze
his crew wrestled line and sail
to gain the weather gauge
at 3 bells of the early watch
two cables off our starboard quarter
the pirates threw a ranging ball
close across our bows
we ran the larboard guns
a few broadsides would allow.

By dawn the breeze had freshened
the sky showed cobalt blue
exchanges had been many
the ending overdue
a 12 lbs. ball cracked her main
a fortunate rendezvous

half a watch she lay wallowing
our cannons barked her doom
the pirate barky went to bottom
with Captain and the crew.

SandyG is retired from Public Safety, he resides in Wayne, New Jersey. "Poetry allows me to share perceptions with the reader. Each poem is a play in which the poet becomes writer, director and actor." Allpoetry.com/SandyG

[Robert Poleski]

Music of the mead

spring's music fills the air
on the surrounding meadow
soil laughs as the flowers ripple
the air pulses
underneath the insect's wings
the music in the sighing of the reed
in the gushing of the rill
wind strikes the chords upon the tree branches
green grasshoppers bounce atop the grass
like leggy trampolines-
lonely calves
bray for company lowing in the mead
witching and sweet
is the music of the hooves
of the horse's iron-shod feet
galloping the lea

overhead-
honking geese- whooping swans
from winter exodus
of banished birds
flowing out of Celtic fairytale
murmuration of starlings
wheel and bank overhead
like wind-tossed gunpowder
an avian aria erupts

from the knot of trees ahead
jays screeching up in the canopy
on the lookout for a feathered meal

faraway on the horizon
silence of the frozen mountains-
earth's silence- throbbing and singing-
breathing of the earth

What I see is my own world, my whole intimate universe, with
my mind, my heart, looking inside things, inside feelings, what
makes it laugh or cry, love or hate, what makes it feel pleasure or
pain. Allpoetry.com/Robert_Poleski

[Laura Sanders]

Everything has its turn

By early August, the purple Vetch is on its way out,
whilst Flea bane arrives in glory, with its golden pout.
Pink Rose- bay Willow, towers tall, just about to seed.
Dry Giant Hogweed burnishes bronze, to dried up weeds.
Ready to drop their ware, to birds passing by,
all the foliage amassed, but picked out, by human eye!
The Teasel heads, display purple florets, fixed on spikes
and the brown heads sway, like candelabra lights!
Even Thistles the pokiest, sharpest of all the plants,
reveal their purple flowers, alone, they stand.
Vetch seeds are now black pods, of a Legume family.
Wild sheep sorrel, is now deep amber, among the green.
Peeping out, among the pink and yellow, is a pure white
trumpet shaped flower, Bindweed, Morning Glory's sight.
Yellow dried field grasses, yearn for quenching rains,
August is a drought month, we will for rain, again!
While thistledown, is set free on currents far and near,
every flower has its turn, in the flowering calendar year.

———————————

I live in a beautiful part of the country, England and take
inspiration from observing nature, people and animals. I enjoy
writing all sorts of poetry . Allpoetry.com/Laura_Sanders.

[Horatio Millin]

Magnolia Dream..

I write of old green houses:
tilted as the pondering
of old men playing dominos
on warped plyboard.

Porch droops with memories
of grandchildren playing hide & seek.
Spiders bounce on their web like trampolines
in the eaves of wilted asphalt shingles;
peeling like dry scabs on old wounds.

The weeping willow trees
wear nests of cardinals like a jewelry;
branches hang low & graceful
as fingers rubbing a balding picket fence
with slats missing like lost teeth.

Yard grass turns brown
with a summer-time cynicism:
patches of ground appear round
& random as spontaneous feline decisions.

The rusty powder-white gate hangs
tilted like a hangover;
half open to a sidewalk as irregular
as a frozen wave.

Old dogs know the geography
of every fire hydrant.

Kids play stickball, & marbles;
skip-ropes blur the air
into a midsummer's sweet
magnolia dream.

Horatio Millin is from St. Thomas, US Virgin Islands. Poetry
helps me record the landscapes of life as seen through eyes of the
heart. Allpoetry.com/talysman

[Bryan Northup]

Mountain made for me

A single elevation,
peak of chicken wire and paper mâché
mounded on a square of particle board
like a science-fair volcano - dormant at last.

Dropped tips of artificial Christmas trees
and dried floral mosses forested the low slopes green
while a faint trail of dust-colored paint led around
to a waterfall of aluminum foil sparkle in a pool

with pebbles and polished rocks Elmer's glued to the bank,
where a family of plastic raccoons washed their food
most nights. There was a steep spot to traverse, a cliff
almost, and if you didn't slip you found the cave -

far too big for this mountain but perfect for
pretending a deer and a horse lived happily there
and were unafraid of the dark or a hibernating bear.
At the summit, frosted white, a chip of obsidian was embedded -

a flat spot for standing and proclaiming
this mountain was made for me.

Bryan is a queer Chicago-based poet and visual artist creating sculptural artwork with discarded materials and reimagined meanings with his words. He is currently working on his first poetry chapbook. Allpoetry.com/Succinctly

[Sandy L Galacio]

Ice!

A sailing ship lifts, pauses, plunges
spray whips along an empty deck
above the bulging main topsail floats
a pale blue translucent bubble
spreading lambent light thru the barky
draping silver chains of ice across her bows

breaks a crescent from the sea
a brighter glow strikes the main tops
liquid silver slides down shrouds and stays
spreads across dampened decking
paints chalk white curls on breaking waves
brightens edges of sailcloth clouds

seamen chant a salty shanty
bare footsteps beat old tattoos
men haul ropes against wind and rudder
tacking ship to starboard
to gain an open view
shrouds tense, sails moan and shudder
she gathers traction
close hauled on her new course

she aims to pass through the frozen sea
and sail for home in roiling waters
gusts betray her, crosscurrents belay her

tossing her on a great frosted iceberg
hull taking water, steerage torn away
rudder lost to a small crevasse
hidden in the cold blue ice

---

78 years young. Poet for two years. Fan of Frost and Cummings
and great admirer of Imagery writ large. Allpoetry.com/SandyG

[Nancy Jackson]

Brandi and the Bunny Rabbit

it wasn't her "teasing the big dogs" voice
nor her running-the-fence raucous uproar
but her "listen up, Mom, come here" bark
"something is wrong and I need you" tone
that gripped my senses that day

rushing to the door I found my chi
yelping beside a dappling striped hare
hastening to their aid I babbled aloud
O Lord, surely she didn't harm that
poor rabbit out there

as I struggled to climb down one steep step
at a time, I winced while watching her drag
her hind legs behind trying to circumvent my
approach toward her, totally unaware
her legs are mirrors of mine

my terrier-chi was shielding the
brownish-white hare, sheltering her
against added impair while
the rabbit's busy bright eye dots
darted from right to left
certain the foe would return

I stooped low and cooed softly
inspecting her fluffy fur coat
no shades of red posed any harm
no open cuts warranted
additional alarm

so I shooed chi-girl upstairs to the house
and carefully observed from the
screened-in porch as the wary
bunny began to relax, cautiously
nibbling lettuce and carrot chip snacks

her nose wiggled gently as she
lazily munched on prickly hay
warming herself on tiny pebbles
sprinkled amongst the petals
and bird seed where she lay

yet failed calls and solitary waits
breathless prayers and pleading texts
soft talk and carrot chips
was all I could offer her
on that fateful day

then through soggy eyes
and gasping sobs I
begged the Lord
to help this tiny
offended one

and now ever etched
into bitter memories is
a sight that reduced me
to weeping furies

the image of a single round
of buckshot
in the back of her
sweet little head

_____

Nancy Jackson grew up by the ocean but now lives in a valley near
the Smokey Mountains. Nature and life experiences frame her
poetry and give voice to her spiritual life and healing journey.
Allpoetry.com/Nancy_daisygirl

[Brian Peter Hodgkinson]

The Bridge Once Lifted

like the very air I breathe
the book's song sings the light
it's the voice standing in back of me
& the center point of this dark world

the pierced hand holds mine
at this sacred footstool of the divine
blood for blood on a carpenter's tree
rusty spikes tacking a crossbeam
riving bones tendons and sinew
hung on the butcher's meat hook

raked with a whip with razor shards
streams of red filming the eyes
needle thorns pin the skull

this, the altar table where
the propitiations' parts laid out
between the firmament's horizon
& this weedy damaged earth
he is now the bridge once lifted

I'm a father of four with seven grandchildren. I lived overseas in Africa and India for over twenty years. I was involved in development work. I love to write and have a graphic imagination. Allpoetry.com/Brian_Peter_Hodgkinson

[Philippe R Hebert]

South East Asia 1965

Sights, sounds, smells
Never before experienced
Still so vivid and intense
After 50 years

So young and venerable
Outwardly brave
Internally quaking
Emotions close to the surface

If anyone knew
That last explosion
You pissed your pants
You're probably not alone

The undergrowth so dense
Humidity so high
No one will notice
'Cause you're soaking wet

Rice paddies terraced
Foot path double as berms
Caribou's pull the plows
Men in PJs and collie hats behind

Women plant rice stems
Both work
From see to can't see
Knee deep in muddy water

The dense ground cover
On the hill side
Sprout red, orange, and coral colored
hibiscus

But Viet Cong move in
At night
Steeling rice and pork
Intimidating all
Interrogating and killing some.

Philippe R. Hebert has written over 50 technical articles that have been published in various technical magazines. He is final negotiations with a publicist for his poetry book "Homage, An Anthology". Allpoetry.com/PRHebert

[Sandy L Galacio]

Resurrection and Redemption

moonlight beaming grey gloom glowing
steep waves roil, sharp winds pull and shove
a sunken ship rises in the raging gale
spray whips along the empty decking

above the bulging main topsail floats
a pale blue translucent bubble
spreading lambent light
through the sodden barky
draping silver chains of ice
across her bows in layered veils

boney ghosts of able seamen
salty sailors dead and pale
man the decks and standing crosstrees
tend the lines and set the sails

jaw bones clicking, chatter clacking
recalling the dragon of the sea
filling canvas full and by
trepidation running free

fire in their boney sockets
reaching hard, listing on the fly
hopeful of redemption
seeking comfort in resurrection

aft to port the hungry dragon wings
stalking oceans, nostrils steaming
spewing brimstone o'er the sea
raiding whale pods rich and teaming
torching fin and toasting gill

attacks from hell in coastal waters
no defense construed
a monster furnace fierce in battle
burning ships and scorching crews
belching smoke and spitting flame

pity more the mighty legend
reduced to myth by fog of time
fearsome dragons evolved to fishes
tiny horses, pretty ponies of the sea

acrobatic humming birds
riding currents in the shadows
spinning pirouettes across the coral reefs
regal facsimiles, fearful dragon brevities
innocents of the deep, lost terrors of the sea
the fiery dragons, monsters of mythology

---

78 years young. Poet for two years. Fan of Frost and Cummings
and great admirer of Imagery writ large. Allpoetry.com/SandyG

[Marta Green]

Scarlet Mountain

the Titan rumbles with a deep base that is ear splitting
like an earthquake, rattling clear panes of glass
framed paintings crashing to the ground
it cracks the foundations and pink stucco walls
eruption warnings sound on the village island

out of the water faucet, comes brown sulphuric acid
smelling like foul rotten eggs
large plumes of steam like a geyser exploding
grey ash falls like snow, obscuring visibility
like a blind man feeling his way through doom

scarlet volcanic rocks descend from the heavens
crashing through roofs of homes
properties, schools, hospitals burning with scalding hot fire
villagers run, bike, drive away from the yawning monster
the main event is just a breath away

deafening explosions as orange liquid lava begins to flow
the mountain is melting like snow turning to slush
a pyroclastic cloud rushes down going hundreds of miles an hour
devouring like a hungry tiger, anything that is in its path
people are evaporated, survivors covered in hanging strips of skin
wails, screams are swallowed up in the mayhem

lava flows slowly reaching the river making a bridge
fluffed red rock, cooling to black volcanic glass
devastation, steadfast islanders that are left vow to rebuild
while others, wither and wash away to new lands
powerful, rumbles reminds that nature is always influx
safety is never guaranteed, islanders are at its mercy

Marta Green is from the great state of Texas where she lives with
her husband. She has three sons and 2 daughters. Her passion has
always been writing, reading and art.
Allpoetry.com/Marta_Green

[Alwyn Barddylbach]

ប្រាសាទបាយ័ន (The Bayon)

I am immortal, protective
of reckless gods and jealous demons,
strangled walls of ancient laterite,
lofty gates crowned with cardinal faces,
contented sentinel of day and night.

I stand reflective, mythopoeic
pillars drowned gleaming in a pristine
buddhist mirror, stillness polished bright -
pilgrimage of virtue, time and places,
plenary of spirits in the morning light.

I scream diurnal and subjective,
lost temple of enigmatic youth,
cyclopaedic tales tossed in stone,
hindu princes, palaces and lotus flowers,
nature's ambience in mystic flight of dawn.

I rest prospective, undiminished
among a riot of figs millstone tight,
elephants in supplication long since gone -
humble bones and calluses, atrium and towers,
mighty jungle city throng of Angkor Thom.

អង្គរធំ

In the heart of Cambodian jungle stands a monument, temple and ancient city c.1190AD – a timeless monolith and civilisation reclaimed by nature; postcard from Angkor, AB 2000.
Allpoetry.com/Barddylbach

[Kim van Breda]

where foliage filters flutter

a desk chair swivels
where foliage filters flutter
on the edge of winged whispers

pewter fluorescence
overhead intractables

as brisk breezes clear
the winter from desktop debris
with silver leaves and peony pleas

green weeps sweet as spearmint
musk infused with plaid pink

paper sheets
clouding skies
window fragrance framed

———————————

With distinctive contemporary style, my pen explores a broad
spectrum, from life experience to short abstract brevity and prose.
All my personal publications available on Amazon.com
worldwide. Allpoetry.com/Mermaid

[Connor Egan]

Shores

once
this land was filled
with fireflies

their small light
flashing like a fat summer
Christmas or some
waist-high constellation

such pretty little stars

the cattails sprout like towers
the spires of the marsh
reaching heights that give
the frogs something to sing about
their croaking, croaking, croaking,
every night an encore of the last

a heron struts
her beak poking beneath pools
graceful legs make ripples
across slivers of streams

Connor (Konreg) Is from Annapolis Maryland. He has been writing poetry on and off for the last 8 years. At 25 he is currently working on his first book of poems. Allpoetry.com/Konreg

[Lydia Austin]

The Churchyard

Silent stone sentinel among the tombs,
Testament to bygone people's pleas.
Here, centuries of contrite voices
Freed tormented minds, while on their knees.

Outside, under the thick green carpet,
Those people lie in infinite sleep.
Life's years etched under weathered lichen
Of stone slabs, planted by those who weep.

Buried yew, now wizened, rise aloft
To shield the ground from the sun's bright blaze.
Re-root, now re-born; this Celtic tree,
A symbol of resurrection praise.

Snowdrops, iris, daffodils grow here,
Dash of colour in this sombre scene.
This abandoned church; this placid nook,
Is more quiet now than it's ever been.

———————————

I am from East Anglia, UK. I currently live near Cambridge with my husband. I write poetry from my inspiration, wherever it takes me. Allpoetry.com/Rosesapling28

[Sasha Logan]

Scent Memories

charred scents linger
within the astronaut's mind
suits, boots, glove fingers
leave scent memories behind
reek of burnt toast and sulfur
a vacuum occupied by scientists and engineers
what Earthly scents trigger
the olfactory bulbs of space pioneers
acid burns, fireworks, the scent of torched meat
the bakery that burns a rack of bagels
on the putrid corner of smelly Smogstone Street
the aromas trigger views from the cosmos
floating in the void
looking down
on the mass of green, tan and blue

Writing random thought. Crime in America is high. Rent in
America is high. You get what you pay for. Living in Michigan.
The less you have, the less you have to deal with.
amazon.com/author/sashalogan Allpoetry.com/Sasha_Logan

[Mister Colvet]

soils of Earth [oars]

we'll paddle our oars
until we run out of starch
and accumulated carbohydrates
our muscles will cease

our bones will ache
but we will eventually heal them
with thick green smoke
dissolving deftly
into the exhaled smog

of a lowly strung
trail of stars
squirming like a bug
over our waxing
whispering campfire flames

and we'll rest our heads
on polypropylene
hydrophobic mummy
sleep bagged sheets

murmuring their
synthetic secrets
and shed particles of sleep
with the meditating
soils of Earth

A plain-clothes engineer, writer, artist, and general over-thinker wrapped into one epithelial sheet deemed human.

Check out my work at lastpagesofhumanity.blogspot.com!
Allpoetry.com/Colvet

[Steven Gelb]

An English Garden

Is a feast for the senses.
There is so much to see, hear, smell and touch.
A Garden of Earthly Delights,
A landscape-painting that comes to life.

We start with a lake whose surface undulates,
With tiny waves upon its shore.
Playful multihued ducks quack joyfully upon its surface.
And the ripples make the ducks,
Bob up and down.

A hilly lawn is a verdant carpet of green.
It is punctuated with flower beds,
And brightly colored blooms.
When we sniff these flowers,
Perfumed fragrances waft through the air.
Busy bumblebees and hummingbirds,
Add a cacophony of sound.

A grove of trees adds stark relief to our garden scene.
The pine trees' needles collect the morning's dew.
Leafy trees attract gaily chirping songbirds.
Lively little squirrels run along the tree trunks.
If we pet them, we feel their soft fluffy coats.
We now must take our leave,
Of this Garden of Earthly Delights

It savored our senses.
It put us in a relaxed mood.
It raised our spirits.
And it readied us to face the world anew.

———————————

An idyllic English Garden
(Hieronymus Bosch, "The Garden of Earthly Delights", Triptych
Oil Painting (circa 1500) El Prado Museum, Madrid, Spain.)

Steven was born in Los Angeles, CA. He enjoys the warm
temperatures and many attractions there. He became interested in
poetry in high school and has continued to feel so to the present
day. Allpoetry.com/Treesky36

[Lydia Austin]

Ghost of Saint Edmund

Among the old abbey ruins
In the deepest part of the night,
Restless, a king's spirit wanders;
A faint spectral shadow of white.

A gold circlet about his head,
Empty scabbard by his left side.
Weathered, bloodstained, tattered garments
Paint his horrific homicide.

The sting of the hard, cold arrows,
Intense pain as his warm blood oozed.
Slaughtered by savage invaders.
'Abandon your god' - he refused.

He scans the cloister, built to him;
A ghost of its powerful past.
Gilded brass gates, the jewels, the art,
Scent of incense and choral chants.

Like the ruined abbey round him,
His bones desecrated, mislaid.
Sainthood abandoned, power lost,
Patronage of England betrayed.

He turns his pale face to the stars
To utter a sorrowful cry.
His sainted shadow slips from sight
As history passes him by.

I am from East Anglia, UK. I currently live near Cambridge with my husband. I write poetry from my inspiration, wherever it takes me. Allpoetry.com/Rosesapling28

[Jessica Orr]

Sunfish

I love many things but
the sunfish shined;
a little lake outside Grandpa's-
yearly trek.

suburban and condos, retired
and stewardship;
his grandkids he showed,
holding reel firm.

bowl haircut and hotdog print shirt,
the fish so fat and flat;
the ducks did argue-
quack, quack.

that photo I still look,
grandpa looking on;
me holding sunfish and
a surprised smile.

––––––––––––

'Nature is so close to Godliness' say Jessica Orr, a 2-book Veteran of the Poetry Genre. Since 2012 she has been writing Poetry & Short Stories. She adores writing! Allpoetry.com/Jessica_Orr

[Marta Green]

Fiery Heat

flickering flames of soft yellow,
traces of red and orange
warmth emanates from a fireplace
we lay down by fiery illusions
on a silky white animal skin rug

my translucent tangerine negligee slowly opens
sparring tongues, slippery and sensual
sweet like citrus crystal drops of nectar
apricot tinged skin from shifting colors like a Van Gough painting

tender touches, clinging, desire
mutually assured pleasure like a kaleidoscope exploding
it is midnight, we fall asleep
listening to the crackle and pop
of a dying blaze

Marta Green is from the great state of Texas where she lives with
her husband. She has three sons and 2 daughters. Her passion has
always been writing, reading and art.
Allpoetry.com/Marta_Green

[Kelsey Jean]

Poetry Is All Around Us

It's in the way his gray eyes gaze at her dotingly
from the opposite edge of the overcrowded chamber,
steadfast and eager – a fresh-faced ship waiting to take sail,
biding time before embarking on his last extraordinary voyage.

It's her lengthy hair cascading across her breasts
as they gently sigh in rhythm to her eager heart beating,
ever so slightly exposed – lit candle in middle of the dancefloor,
humbly anticipating the charmed advance of one fine suitor.

The way the calculated bartender pours two brimming flutes
replenished with bubbling citrus as he surveys intently
the two sightly strangers – a deliciously potent potion,
sent off with both names attached, to intertwine fate and reality.

It's the elderly couple fondly reminiscing with admiration
at magic as it delicately unfolds before their skilled watchful eyes,
old boy gently nudging his wife to muster – soldiers deployed,
displaying steadfast love, they sway betwixt the young pair.

Or the stars radiating from agape rooftop fashioning spotlights
that illuminate the suddenly flushed pair of captivated guests,
declaring them as the night fades away – moon's hushed lullaby,
guiding their timid and desiring glances to meet at long last.

Kelsey Jean is from Owatonna, Minnesota. For her poetry has often been the most perfect escape. Without poetry, there is no water to replenish or air to breathe - without it there is no life. Allpoetry.com/Kelsey_Jean

[Mia Emily]

Captain Crawl

a spectacled young man, tall and thin
had a strawberry beard covering his chin
he was master of his ship from stem to stern
when he hurt his bones, a little down the skeleton

now hunched over in such incredible pain
his crew had to come up with a brand-new name
crawling about from starboard to port
he no longer looked tall, but certainly looked short

with a new image to uphold, it was no wonder
since rather than walking over he had to crawl under
despite being so tall, he was always on the ground
Captain Crawl has become the shortest sailor around

Mia Emily is from the east coast of Malaysia. She is a professor at MARA University of Technology. She is also a writer who still struggles to write her own biography. Allpoetry.com/Mia_Emily

[Alwyn Barddylbach]

Tuppence Torn

Charmed orbs of circumstance
and sweet contention, sky twisters
stardust wings of flame -
no mention of their name.
Transient heartbeat unlamented,
nature's call come furtive
madly glancing.

Fate obscured by cloud and storm,
not a nickel spilt, swift flight
gentle face, grave we fall -
trick or spite, fleeting thought, a treat.
Vanish quickly watch me spin,
pure without a beat or trace
nonsense bite.

Wee quantum tusk and tall,
selfless lure of dusk and dawn,
mischief or brave intention -
perpendicular phantom trance,
heart of pity chance embrace.
Swell on mountain ocean
in absence dance.

I know a secular life, time
and place, worlds this small

caves that barely yawn -
fiery rills on dust blown trails,
natural springs ventricular sails.
Nonesuch pass these twilight walls
brilliance falls.

Puff of blossom starry cluster,
misty dales, lions whimper
angels weeping -
whereto the faithful gather,
mad dogs and tigers leaping.
Far below the canyon crawl
giants whisper.

Green hills so far away,
ever blue, breath upending
skies unborn, uplifting thunder -
tear me from your feet asunder.
Singularity, ascension,
whirl and fame, circumstance
tuppence torn.

Through the roaring waters plunder,
through the silky sapphire spray
defiance temper storm -
to our maker make no mention
deafened by our mansion sway.
But loveliest of all for ever
once contented...

Once for ever
all is done, moon suspended
curtains drawn.

Standing on a rock, close to the edge, surge of magic running through those veins. Living in a place of fate where others fear to tread, we know the way but we don't tell - AB Blue Mountains. Allpoetry.com/Barddylbach

[Lorrie West]
Thanksgiving dinner

Well another year Thanksgiving
Dinner Turkey and ham for the
Meats mash potatoes and sweet
Potatoes carrots and green beans
For the trimmings delicious cranberry
Sauce on the side desert apple pie
Cherry pie for that freshly taste of a
Thanksgiving dinner God bless

My name is Lorrie Ann McConnell-west I write poetry for fun
I've been writing for years now started in my twenties I'm fifty-
five years old I have three children which have grown I live in
Michigan Allpoetry.com/lorrie_west

[Jenni Taylor]
Evergreen Tree

The Evergreen foliage stays green all year round
keeping hold of its verdure through all seasons
retaining its relevance, popularity, and usefulness
showing its sharp and spiky needles
different size pinecones falling to the ground
continuously fresh or self-renewing
housing birds of all kinds and colors
with brown edgy bark peeling away
it's twigs and branches used for decoration
may become holly, like mistletoe and ivy
or Christmas trees presenting lights and ornaments
colorful wrapping paper hugging presents underneath
remaining perennial fresh, interesting, or well-liked
time to present itself to all those around

Due to a car accident in 2002, I am paralyzed from the neck down and vent dependent. Most of my poems are about me, my accident, hope, gratitude, for contests and life in general. Allpoetry.com/Jtay

[John Wilhite]

The Blind Date

elated, when I first saw you four our blind date,
attraction tightened my stomach
tall, salt and pepper hair, wavy, touching shirt collar
glacial blue eyes looking into my chocolate ones

your large warm hand is placed on the small of my back
leading like a shepherd protecting me into a restaurant
can't take my eyes off of your masculine body
body of a weight lifter, full pectorals like two tight breasts
aquiline nose, perfect kissable lips, strong chin

sharing beef fajitas, tender white flour tortillas made from scratch
caramelized brown onions, green peppers, red tomatoes
guacamole, sour cream cold and silky, Pico De Gallo
the taste of grilled meat strips with toppings explodes in our
mouths
drinking top shelf sweet Margaritas
licking some salt of the crystal bulbous glass

talking, finding you are kind, honest, brave and funny
smiling, white even teeth are like a walk in the moonlight
holding my hand gently as you tell me
"You are so beautiful"

I blush like a pink rose, my dark onyx long hair hides my eyes
lifting my chin, "I'm serious, don't you know?"

finishing dinner, going out to Starbucks for a hot chocolate mocha
we talk for hours, getting to know the things we have in common

your incredible Artic vivid sea blue orbs look inside me
can't take my gaze away from you as you lean to kiss me
taking my breath away, I could fall at your feet
worshiping the God of loveliness who knows not what he does to me

back at my mountain cabin, he again brushes his softness against me
hoping I will see you again, memorized by your handsomeness

Marta Green is a Southern writer who is passionate about poetry, family, reading, writing and art. She lives in Texas with her 3 sons, 2 step daughters, and 5 grandchildren!
Allpoetry.com/Marta_Green

[Jim Beitman]

waves

the power of waves
is much greater than mine
as It rounds off the rocks
slowly over time
captivated by the motion
and drunken by its potion
of salted mist and sunset kissed
colors of aqua blue and green
rolling under the surface
humming the song of the sea
performing proudly just for me

I am an artist living in Noblesville Indiana. Writing is a great media that helps distill my feelings, thoughts, and experiences. It is always a great thrill to be included in an Allpoetry anthology! Allpoetry.com/Beitmanjim

[Paul Goetzinger]

The Frozen Lake

At the corner of Peabody Road
Near the base of a hill
There is a flooded pasture
Surrounded by forests of pine
As winter descends upon the hidden gem
The miracle of Mother Earth gives birth
To a frozen lake
The mirror of trees and sky
Reflector of the sun
With icy panoramas

On the west shore perches a hemlock
Its woody figure shrouded
In a majestic palace of ice
On the lake surface
Cluttered stones of all sizes
Eroded and fallen from the nearby hill
Frozen sentinels, now embedded, immovable from their positions
While ice shards gather on its pristine shores
Like pieces of glass from the arctic tundra

In the far distance comes a sound
Of all humanity loving things wintry
Frozen war has been declared
Between teenagers
Piles of skates, sticks, gloves and helmets
A game of lake-hockey

No boards or lines
No cup to be won
Two tree branches strung together
With old fishing net for goals
Fixed in the soil on opposite ends of the rink
Neighborhood honor to the victor

The faceoff
A puck is dropped and takes flight
A disorganized rush of adolescent puberty gives chase
Skating furiously on legs of unsure balance
One escapes the Newtonian bonds of the frozen surface
Soaring upward towards the heavens
Falling to earth with a tremendous crash
As the sound of a Star Wars laser echoes off the hillside
Freezing shoreline observers
Like newborn fawns in tall grass

The little war proceeds
Far into dusk
Arms and legs struggle in a flurry of hurried combat
To one side and the other
For supremacy of the cherished black orb
As light snow flurries invade from the east
A player knocks a goalie from his feet
Receives the pass
She scores
Celebration ensues

Frustration commences
Arguments of unfair play and violations of ethics

The puck, launches across the lake
Flung in rage
Gaining speed on the undisturbed ice
Frantic screams echo through the valley
A pond of migratory ducks
Huddled in open water for warmth
Flee towards the sky in terror

As the black object approaches
It slows to a halt
On the edge of the thin, unsteady flow
Giving hope to assembled millennials
Of a miracle on ice
But alas, the lip of ice breaks away
The puck slips under the waves
Disappearing into the grasp of the eerie, cold darkness
Never to see light until summer

Stunned silence settles over the landscape
Game over, the rink is closed
Crowds depart for warmer environments
As winter places the frozen lake
Back into the arms of nature's white pastel|

Paul Goetzinger is a freelance writer and educator from Des Moines, Washington. He has written articles for magazines and other publications for the past 19 years.
Allpoetry.com/Paul_Goetzinger

[J Duke Beall]

Farrier

The moon is slipping
between the clouds
shy of the star-speckled crowds

She poses as a clipping
a crescent sliver trimmed
from some audacious hoof
that left the dippers dimmed
as it trotted with its sisters
far above earth's glimmering roof
carrying a bright celestial ungulate

Who forgot to close the milky gate?

Duke is from Alexandria, VA. She often resorts to "inertia poetry" where she writes as quickly as she can to evade her perfectionist kill-joy inner critic. Allpoetry.com/JDB23

[Melvie Gomez]

3-Fold Utopian Dream

Beams in as soft breeze smoothly blows the sheers,
rays of light dispersed like peaking sun.
Underneath the silk, I turned, to the window I gazed,
zoned out in the clatter of the waves and fronds.

That aroma of my favorite bag of beans
A cup of pleasure on the kitchen counter
Wakes me up from the abyss to a beautiful scene
My man in an apron, cooking eggs, humming with the flipper.

The kids chuckle outside, they ditched their cereals halfway.
Their giggles and smiles, shows the purest.
Swinging in the cadence, smooth sail
On the couch by the porch I sit, there I write best.

Shallow this may seem..
For me, it's a 3-fold Utopian dream.

Filipina living in Dubai. I find it difficult voicing out what I feel.
My poetry is my release.

A monochromatic soul in a vibrant world.

This is my form of expression. This is me.
Allpoetry.com/bornsoltera

[Rachel K. Martin]

Chips Amigos

Triangular crack-offs of flat corn chips
made for guacamole, sour cream, or salsa dips
adding smooth melted cheese
on them please!
just a spicier chip than the dull ones
add seasoning from the bag to the big dull ones
swimming at the bottom of a bag
they make reaching hard to pull it out of the bottom of a bag
coated my fingers with cheese trying to with a coughing gag
sucked on them like it wasn't these fingers
how will it be such a place is made for the chip zingers
at the store next to flavorless pieces of bread
more than a plenty in a bag
they are much more than the rag
that got sprinkles on them
and that mac and cheese, dang'm!
that washed it down with a cup of fresh spring water
Chips make amigos of goods to barter

The poet's name is Rachel K. Martin. She graduated from Saint
Louis University with a B.A. in English and from Webster
University with a M.A. in Patent Agency.
Allpoetry.com/BlueAngelıııı

[Marta Green]

The Unending Ocean

industrial trading ships move out of port to unknown
destinations
an old wooden cargo ship rides waves up
like climbing a steep watery mountain
then down, splashing like roiling pots of water
rain falls in sheets, an angry spray of salt

a fair wind slowly blow storm clouds north
as sun beams peek through a rainbow
a translucent arch of blue, purple, green, red, orange and yellow
you navigates through calm Asian waters
after reaching Japan, unloading box cars,
it will be a timeless journey back to the Americas

kismet, locating each other by chance on line
slowly finding out information about each other
our age, seventeen years your senior
becoming fast friends
we have not seen each other in person
only photographs give us a vision of the untouchable

hearing silent voices through words typed
a romance blooms like undulating green sea grasses
within the confines of the clear blue frothy ocean

seven hours apart
you are in darkness sleeping soundly when I am in morning light
texting, sometimes meeting in the middle where it is personal
excited to visualize and fantasize about soft lips kissing

declarations of love, are they real or an illusion?
how can a people become passionate bound by sea and land
living in different countries, Germany and Texas in the U.S.A.
a Houston apartment awaits your return home
home is longing for sound, scents of cooking, a comfortable bed

I am to meet you in person when you land the behemoth of a ship
at the Houston Port Authority
what will happen in that moment?
will land and sea barriers disappear?
can a language barrier be breached?

I see you, dressed in white,
with gold captain insignias on shoulders
in shiny black shoes carrying a cargo bag with belongings
recognizing you from a photo online
hesitantly, I start walking on the old wooden pier
scared that our love was just imagined

you see me and wave heartily
a white smile with brown eyes shining like stars
seem to make my doubts disappear
like a door has been opened
cobwebs of doubt melt away

running to each into each other's arms
hello and hallo, each in our native tongues

Marta Green is from the great state of Texas where she lives with her husband. She has three sons and 2 daughters. Her passion has always been writing, reading and art.
Allpoetry.com/Marta_Green

[Dino Andino]

The Creature from The City Of Lamps

Inside this city of lamps
where buildings are appealing and hold the sky
I divulge it feels empty most of the time.
Despite the mortal mess, cars, or soda cans.

There's always a stranger without a home
or a lone wolf within the pack.
A face distorted in the shimmering lights.
Some sort of creature of the night
towards me, you walked
with a rucksack full of oaths
quantities of curious something
but you are running out of time.

Daylight is his adversary
heart dwells in the dark
He is frightened by the waters
although the fish is his zodiac sign.

And now you are just a legend
a myth we write about
the lore is about you and the chaos that walks with you.
The fable of the city lamps enunciates that
to keep your eyes away one must always have
-a candle, a blessing, and this poem in hand.

Andino is from Brooklyn, NY. He w to the Pontifical Catholic University of Puerto Rico where he completed a bachelor in Fine Arts and a Minor in Psychology. 'I commit to paper the things I cannot air' Allpoetry.com/Andino

[Nicole Morrish]

No Victim Here

It is time
to fly to a higher branch
release feathers, open
to beckon the storm to obliterate
the last pieces of this shredded self
let your longing, lead
unbury yourself
put back your broken pieces
clench your fists
and scream
shout
howl to the spirits gathering around you
subdued, not me, I'm not subdued
dimmed, not me
take up space
glow a most fierce light

Nicole Morrish is from Nederland, Colorado. Poetry helps me cope with everything and allows me room in my soul to feel it all. I am also an Artist living my always meandering path. Allpoetry.com/Nicole_morrish

[Rachel K. Martin]

Blizzard Battles

Cold air consumes their skulls
cracking and shattering, shards hang loosely together
as the hats hug the heads shut
the sun shuts its eye on a white light patch
a whirlwind of cold gray crystalline pierces the jaws
chaffed skin forms into soars
bodies collapse under the up-swept wind currents
buried in icy graves, the men fight for release

The poet's name is Rachel K. Martin. She graduated from Saint Louis University with a B.A. in English and from Webster University with a M.A. in Patent Agency.
Allpoetry.com/BlueAngelιιιι

[Joseph Hugh Kitchens III]
The Tiny Bird

A tiny bird stood on a branch in no man's land,
Where the mud is weaker than flan
And the skeletons of trees reach up like old turkey bone,
"Life, sweet life, where have you gone? Please come back."
The tiny bird said,
but only the moldy dead were audient.

Hiker, Historian, Bicyclist, Medievalist, Gaming and Cinema
Enthusiast, Amateur Cartoonist, native of South Georgia USA,
now living in the wonderful state of Colorado USA.
Allpoetry.com/JHK3

[Katherine Michaels]

The Other Side of Snow

Stillness weaves upon this mountain
a mantle white with satin snowfall,
misting my search through flake-born fountain
to whispers of your footsteps' call.

Where did you walk in wintry wonder
amidst the white-gloved forest fingers?
I touch your trail as nestled under,
but hold your emblazoned tread still lingers.

Because you've crossed ice-crystalled prism,
I feel warm breath when cold winds blow,
and know we'll emerge in colored-ray rhythm
upon the other side of snow.

Katherine Michaels, a native Texan, writes to celebrate the beauty,
impact, and impression of words. She seeks to paint vivid word-
pictures and share their mysterious effect.
Allpoetry.com/memory_trace

[S. Libellule]
Cattails in the Gloaming

Now is another bewitching hour
with all of its power
time trapped between day and night
not quite dark yet not quite light
anointed with a pink and purple hue

The cattails stand guard
stand their lonely post
thin, black and straight
sentinels at the temporal gate

Bearing witness to the time
when prose becomes rhyme
when fact becomes metaphor
as whispers appear
in voices so clear
having finally found a home
in the warm chill of the gloam

Originally from New England, Libellule currently lives outside of
Birmingham, Alabama. Poetic influences include Mary Oliver,
Billy Collins and ee cummings. Allpoetry.com/Little_Dragonfly

[Lydia Austin]

Winter Fog

Fluffed, white blanket cloaks the land,
The veil of fog covers all.
Above, dark grey shadows loom;
Roofs, trees, towers, lost in mist.
Ahead, the flat grey road fades;
Distance eaten by grey murk.

Frost lingers on the pavements
And dusts brave spider's bare webs.
Birds totter on iced water
Under the faint, pale white disk.
Tree skeletons reach over
As ice clings to each surface.

Shiver under thick layers,
Cocoon hands in padded gloves.
Warm breath writhes as white ether
In the frosty, foggy air.

I am from East Anglia, UK. I currently live near Cambridge with my husband. I write poetry from my inspiration, wherever it takes me. Allpoetry.com/Rosesapling28

[Robert Poleski]

Children of the Sun

the sun shines-
ignites world with a brilliance
we his children
the star dust folks
showered in the dazzling white-
seeking water in the valley of springs
come through the cloud and mist
the silent shadows
look up for the answers

after a lifetime of regrets
run away from who we really are
fly on waxed wings
look for the light to outshine the sun
quench the knowledge thirst
with tears of the earth
before night fall comes
darkness falls and eats us-
devours us alive

we are the children of the sun
dissonant in darkness-
we are meant to shine
disperse the clouds
dress in sparks and light
and dance with the sun

in the glory of splendor in the grass
return home
where all started
make our own way

What I see is my own world, my whole intimate universe, with
my mind, my heart, looking inside things, inside feelings, what
makes it laugh or cry, love or hate, what makes it feel pleasure or
pain. Allpoetry.com/Robert_Poleski

[Laney Leighanne]

Her Cavern

A cave with no entrance.
a hollowed-out hole
in a mountain.
That mountain built with
tears as flowing waterfalls
aged bruises the color of grass and sunflowers
clay resembling the blood dripping down ones hands.
the multitude of sandy spots, showing a glimmer of stress
the small cliffs and holes proving past weathering.

A hollowed hole within
holding the new
clay.
Holding the growing
sunflowers.
Watching the water
drip through and onto
her.

She lay there
limp but breathing softly
still but shaking slightly
naked but not vulnerable.
Remember?
The cave has no entrance.

I am from Longview, TX. I've written since my father passed last year; I'm only 18, poetry has created a therapeutical outlet for me as I've learned about myself. I do so between softball and class. Allpoetry.com/laneyleighanne

[Kelsey Jean]

Entirely Enamored

Completely captivated by you and content to eternally swim
within the gentle cloudy seas of your pearl gray eyes
and to be sun-kissed by your pillowy pliant lips – a palate
reminiscent of toasted oak barreled bourbon and vanilla;
your aromatic aura of spiced sandalwood and lush bamboo
leaves me in weak-kneed rhapsody.

The delicious run of my extremities through your thick
Amerindic mane, across your chest and down your wolfy trails
pleasantly prickles you with sensation – a deep-rooted uproar.
Spellbound by every exclusive impression and adored mannerism
I surrender myself to the core of your affection for all the days of
my life.

Kelsey Jean is from Owatonna, Minnesota. For her poetry has
often been the most perfect escape. Without poetry, there is no
water to replenish or air to breathe - without it there is no life.
Allpoetry.com/Kelsey_Jean

[Steven Gelb]

The Grand Canyon's Natural Glory

The sun rises above the Grand Canyon's rim
Like the blaze of one million spotlights.
It puts an end to the barrenness
Of hundreds of morning shadows
Looking as jagged as the mountains of the moon.

Day progresses to high noon
When the sun shines directly downward.
Suddenly the stillness of noontime is shattered,
By a thunderstorm producing
A torrential downpour with thunder
Like the pounding of anvils.
Zeus hurls lightning bolts from the top of Mount Olympus.
But as soon as the storm appeared
It rapidly retreats to the east
Blown by favorable winds and downdrafts
Within the mystic canyon's walls.

Finally, the sun has reached day's end.
Its rays peek furtively through the crevices
Atop the canyon's walls.
Another day in the Grand Canyon's life has passed
Another one of the countless others
That have placed mortal humans
In awestruck worship and amazement.

Steven was born in Los Angeles, CA. He enjoys the warm
temperatures and many attractions there. He became interested in
poetry in high school and has continued to feel so to the present
day. Allpoetry.com/Treesky36

[Brad Fitzsimmons]
Seed in The Wind

grandiose thoughts reach the sky
far above cares and worries sure
every corpse abhorrent boor
eagle's eyes perceive
what I will receive
mustard seed form miniscule
taken from humanity's cesspool
planted battlefields crimson sea
mustard seed towers now a tree
and all the birds nest in it their home
for the great no longer roam

I'm from Indiana and my calling in life is all poetry. I'm 61 years
old and enjoy reading and writing.
Allpoetry.com/Brad_Fitzsimmons

[Pattimari Sheets Cacciolfi]

Rebirth

Behind the house today
I cut away tall, slender stems
out near the bay
lugging away dead leaves
dry and old
moist earth stoked my soul
Meditative moments rapped my mind
colors of bright with eternal glory
shifted my sting away
Black decaying rot loosened my weakness
Fresh baby buds
were born today
Thirst lush
with water drizzling
roots growing
reminded me of hope
gathered
place in beds of color
timid stride
with worries in forgotten days
Rain draws near
leaving dampness

The garden will be filled with power
packed with love
wonderment singing

always budding
with each change
Merit!

_____

She dances to the tune
of her drummer
sings
to people around
encouraging
always
intuitiveness
is high
spirits
happy
positive over negative

Allpoetry.com/Pattimari

[Felisa Jenlins]

Number & Name

Flipped the pages of black and white.
BOOM! - in the middle
Red sharpie of an azure wound
Umbilical cord
Temptation coursed
Respiratory hitches.
Stealthy crumbled
Tossed aside.
Alas a
Glowering ruddy eye
Mugging me.
Blindly, thru salted rivers
Confetti below my feet.
Memory abolished

Single woman living in Texas. I've been writing poetry since I was a pre- teen. It's a catharsis for me to deal with many negative emotions and trauma I've experienced in my life.
Allpoetry.com/Broken_Vessel

[J R Williams]

Hair Petals

You are like a garden rose, blowing in the breeze
Fiery hair flowing like bright petals making you stand out
Soft eyes gleaming like morning dew drops glistening in sunlight
Stems that seem strong and firm, always keeping you upright
There are other flowers but the way your petals fall past your
leaves
I'd pick you if it weren't for your thorns
I am afraid to bleed
And though it may be pleasant placing you beside me
I prefer to shelter myself from the pain
Flowerless and only observing from afar

Writing has been the most effective way of expressing myself, as
I'm sure many others can relate. I'm very excited to have this
opportunity to share that with you. Allpoetry.com/J.R._William

[Lonna Lewis Blodgett]

The Holding At Laguna Creek

The narrow trail led down from the ridge
Steadying my gait to cling to the steep side
Each step piloting a visionary descent on this secluded land bridge
Quenching this heart with wild undisturbed splendor with every
stride

Pivoting beams of radiant sun flashed
Through the sea green dresses of resplendent trees
Descending to the far woodland floor towards the water's cache
Where the crashing river of water over rock sets Nature's spirit
free

Gilded sunlight lifts each footstep through this fervent forest
when
This pathfinder stops to capture a moment in the muted hush
Coming to rest from this journey to find himself destined
To reside where the forest grows silent and lush

Poised within the mind's communal well
Where the spirit thirsts to feel Nature's endless streams unwrap
There lies something timeless where eternity dwells
Transcending our path to simply find the gap
Between the connection of our soul
And the ingredients of our map

I have spent my lifetime searching for answers regarding truth, purpose and meaning. Poetry is the quintessential conveyance intrinsic to the definition of the human experience. It is written art. Allpoetry.com/Lonna_Lewis_Blodgett

[Jim Beitman]

driftwood

we are driftwood
carved by the ocean's
unending salty motion
into organic
shapes and attitudes
that we present to the world
once we are born on the shore

I am an artist living in Noblesville Indiana. Writing is a great
media that helps distill my feelings, thoughts, and experiences. It
is always a great thrill to be included in an Allpoetry anthology!
Allpoetry.com/Beitmanjim

[Connor Egan]

On stealing my heart

Take my wheat and drink my wine
darling, you share your light
and the world knew spring
I am just a man
I know not all the answers and
I cannot slay the dragons that fester

but I do know of love
I know that you, holy one
have stolen from my chest
keep my heart close
let the warmth touch your skin
it will whisper to you all the love
I have held for you inside
It speaks of the sky
how all the stars and space between
are just imitations of the freckles
that paint your back
how the tide returns to the shore
just to kiss the ground beneath your feet
how the earth bends for you

you, royal one
your court has lay siege to my chest
and as my walls crumble beneath your touch
I am but a boy again

climbing the parapet waving the white flag
surrendered to you
darling, take my wheat and drink my wine
feast on the love I have for you
you, my eden
a never-ending spring

Connor (Konreg) Is from Annapolis Maryland. He has been
writing poetry on and off for the last 8 years. At 25, he is currently
working on his first book of poems. Allpoetry.com/Konreg

[Lily Byrne]

The Ocean's Love Song

In the depths of the ocean blue
Where sunlight fades and darkness ensues there
Lies a world untouched by man,
A realm of mystery and magic grand.

Wails of whales and songs of sirens
Echo through the vast expanse of silence where
Creatures unknown to human eyes,
Glide through the water with grace and surprise.

The coral reefs, a colorful array
A canvas painted by nature's way it's
Teeming with life, a symphony of sound,
A wonderland to be found.

But as we venture deeper still
Into the abyss, a world so chill a
Darkness engulfs, a cold embrace,
And fear grips our hearts in this eerie space.

Yet even here, life does exist
Adapting and surviving in this abyss is
A reminder of nature's resilience,
And the power of adaptation and persistence.

And so we contemplate, in awe and wonder
The mysteries of this world down under lies
A testament to the beauty and power,
Of our planet, a precious, irreplaceable tower.

As we delve deeper into this realm unknown
We find that life takes on a different tone where
Glowing creatures, luminescent and bright,
Illuminate the depths, a magical sight.

Strange and surreal, the world down under
A reflection of nature's infinite wonder and yet
as we journey further still,
We cannot help but feel a sense of thrill.

For in this mysterious world
A reminder of our insignificance and the grand design we find
A realization that we are but a small part,
Of a greater whole, a work of art.

And so we ponder the mysteries of this world
The secrets it holds, the stories untold the
Lessons it teaches, the wisdom it imparts,
As we strive to protect it with all our hearts.

For as we explore and discover this abyss
We must remember that it is not ours to miss rather
A gift that we must cherish and preserve,
For generations to come, for all to observe.

And so we dive into the depths of the sea
In search of the wonders that are meant to be a
Journey of discovery, a quest for truth,
A deepening of our love for this planet, forsooth.

As we explore the depths of the sea
We are reminded of our fragility for
In this world so different from our own,
We are but guests, on this journey alone.

We witness the effects of human interference
A destruction wrought without any preference for
Coral reefs, once teeming with life,
Now a graveyard, a sign of our strife.

And yet, there is still hope to be found
A chance for redemption, to turn things around we
Learn from nature's resilience and power,
And vow to protect, in this crucial hour.

We dive deeper still, with a sense of purpose
To uncover the secrets of this underwater surface we
Marvel at the ingenuity of each creature,
A lesson in adaptation, a natural feature.

And as we ascend towards the surface
We carry with us a newfound purpose to
Protect and preserve, with all our might,
This precious planet, a beacon of light.

For in the depths of the ocean blue
We find a connection, both old and new a gift
To the world around us, and to each other,
A reminder of our common mother.

And so we pledge, to protect and serve
This planet, our home, with a steadfast nerve and promise
To cherish and nurture, with all our might,
The wonders of this world, both day and night.

And so we emerge from the depths of the sea
With a newfound sense of responsibility to
Take care of this planet, our only home,
And ensure that its beauty forever roams.

For the mysteries of the ocean, deep and vast
Are but a small part of a world that's vast from
The forests to the deserts to the skies,
Our planet is a treasure, beyond any prize.

And yet, we have taken it for granted for too long
Assuming it will always be here, forever strong,
But the signs are clear, and the warnings dire,
Our actions threaten to set the world on fire.

So we must act now, with a sense of urgency
To protect and preserve, with all our capacity to
Make changes, both big and small,
And ensure that our planet will stand tall.

For in the depths of the ocean blue
We have learned the lessons that are true of
Resilience, adaptation, and survival,
And the importance of our planet's revival.

So let us take a pledge, a vow
To live in harmony with nature, somehow to
Reduce our impact, to heal and restore,
To protect the planet that we adore.

For in the depths of the ocean blue
We have found a connection, both old and new to the
World around us, and to each other,
A reminder of our common mother.

And so we stand at the crossroads, my friend
With the future of our planet, in our hands to tend we
Can choose to continue on the path we're on,
Or take the road less travelled, to a brighter dawn.

For in the depths of the ocean blue
We have found a love, both deep and true for
The wonders of this planet, both near and far,
And the need to protect it, like a shining star.

So let us take this love, and let it guide our way
As we work towards a brighter, more sustainable day for
The mysteries of the ocean, and the beauty of the land,
Are a testament to the power of our human hand.

Let us cherish and preserve, with all our might
This precious planet, our only home and delight for
In the depths of the ocean blue,
We have found a connection, both old and new.

A connection to the world around us, and to each other
A bond that unites us, like no other and
With this bond, we can forge ahead,
Towards a future where our planet is always well-fed.

So let us take this journey, with purpose and grace
And work towards a world, that we can all embrace for
In the depths of the ocean blue,
We have found a love, both old and new.

———————————

Lily is a young poet from the Gold Coast, Australia. She is
currently a student, pursuing her passion for literature and
creative writing through her studies, and her growing anthology.
Allpoetry.com/L._Sarah

[Mohammed Ali]

Why are you back?

You said "I love you"
And my heart bloomed with joy anew
But now you're back, and I wonder why
Has your lover left, or do you just feel lonely inside?

I was always there, by your side
But you chose not to wait, and my love you denied
Remember when I gave you my all
But you held back, and my heart did fall

What's different now, why are you back?
Did you truly love me, or just filling a lack?

I loved you with every flaw and scar
My beloved, I loved you even when you hated who you are
I longed to talk to you, despite speaking little with others
I waited for you, even when waiting was a bother

Remember when I travelled miles to see your face
Hoping to find happiness in your embrace
But your reception was cold, and in your eyes I saw indifference
I knew then that to you, my love made no difference

My beloved, why are you back now?
Is it love you seek, or just a sense of how?

Remember when you were just ordinary to them
But to me, you were everything, every little gem
Why did you choose someone else over me?
I was ready to give you gardens while they only offered a tree

Does he give you a flower when I would give you an entire field?
Did his money defeat me when I was ready to share everything I yield?
Tell me, why are you back now when you are still attached to his memory?
I know he still lives in your heart with a love that's contrary

I apologize, but my heart no longer trusts you
I apologize, for my ribs can't bear the pain anew
I apologize, for I can no longer be your reserve
But know this, my love will never swerve

After time and years, you'll know who I am
The true friend, lover, husband, and father I am
But alas, life's too short to make you stumble back into my arms
My love for you will always stay true, but it's time to move on
from these harms.

I struggled to express myself, and words would not appear, but
poetry found me and gave my feelings a clear sphere.
Allpoetry.com/Dudu_96

[Makaylar Tatiana Georgina Angel-Shim]

Secret Mystic

Candy coloured cloud
It's a sand cloud rainbow
Colour kylie sky
this place that will astound you.
With multicolour roses, tulip's
Flowers
Pink rain falls in the heat
Of the red sun in abundance.
Trees that are amazing.
That has all the fruit
What you have never seen
The mystic secret
An endless garden world.
As the gentle breeze
That ripples the little stream.
That reflects the mirror image
Of the candy kylie sky
That magnificence of delight.
An. Incredible remarkable place
For who are worthy
A God-given gratification.
From heaven

Stay with me, nobody knows.
The way I feel. Why, what have I done wrong.
I try my best to live in a right way.
So when I talk to my sisters.
Let them feel no way.
Allpoetry.com/CherubimSeraphim

[Richard E Thomas]
Don't be deceived

The morning sun is rising
On the frozen frosted ground
The birds are quiet and silent
Even a pin drop echoes with sound.

The trees standing naked
And a breeze it nips the air
It's a time of recollection
To understand the love we share.

So as the sun melts the frost
The frost vanishes without a trace
Appreciate the silent birds
As the trees show you to embrace.

Embrace the people around you
Be thankful for the love received
Remember the world doesn't care
So see clearly, don't be deceived.

Hi I'm 46, father of 7 lovely girls and have worked as a support
worker for over 20 years and my writing helps me get through life
without too much stress it has also helped me connect to other
people. Allpoetry.com/Richard_E_Thomas

[Kristi Weber-Suarez]

Shreds

Tattered shreds of dignity
In my white knuckled fist
I watch my world implode
As your taillights fade away

Choking back the tears
I stifle another scream
As the cell door slams home
History repeats itself

Should I run, can I hide
The nightmare of my existence
Threatens to consume my soul
Guilt decided by a jury of one

You alone decided my fate
As I frantically ripped the pages
Hoping for an alternate ending
But condemnation ruled

Now an empty vessel, I turn away
Last shred of dignity at my feet
And I step away into the night
A worthless soul with vacant eyes

Born in Ohio and raised in Florida, my sister & mother instilled a love of the spoken word deep in my soul. My family, both past & present, inspire my poetry... every word is a piece of my heart. Allpoetry.com/Kristi_Weber

[Jacob Gardner]

Into the Water

There's a stranger who keeps coming to my house,
In threadbare shoes and a cotton blouse.
I would ask him what he wants,
But he's already inside,
Amber from the candlelight.

And he sleeps in my bed -
The first time I've done something so, so clandestine.
He removes his shirt,
I remove his ring,
I'm filled with chagrin.

Wrapped in sheets, he leads me out the door,
We've attempted this once before,
Leaving the entrance wide awake.

It's cold outside, entering winter.
The moonlight synchronizes with the tide,
The waves shimmering with the hue of snow.

I see the ghost of him again.
He whispers, "Come into the water,"
And so I do, nothing to lose.
The salty water stings,
Invectives evaporate from my skin and

Rise to the surface above,
While I sink until I'm met with the sycamore trees.

There, high in the branches, rests
The all too familiar phantom, and I am reminded
There is a reason I've trekked this path once before.

There's a stranger who keeps coming to my house,
In threadbare shoes and a cotton blouse.
He tells me that I'm a lamb to the slaughter.
"I'm already dead," I reassure him -

I've already gone into the water.

Jacob Gardner, residing in Sarasota, Florida, has been writing
since his elementary years. Outside of writing, his passion
illuminates in both music and fashion. Jacob Gardner also loves
fruit. A lot. Allpoetry.com/Jacob_Gardner

[S. Libellule]

Arboreal

It is this time of year
that I truly notice
that I again witness
these silent sentinels

How they stand so
tall...
denuded of leaves
yet ever commanding

Almost demanding
an arboreal respect
earned ring by ring
while the decades sing

As they hold up
our very world
everything unfurled
moment by moment

Their bark is cracked deep
scarred by the seasons
for so many reasons
like some secret braille

Originally from New England, Libellule currently lives outside of Birmingham, Alabama. Poetic influences include Mary Oliver, Billy Collins and ee cummings. Allpoetry.com/Little_Dragonfly

[Kenneth Canatsey]

A humble little centipede

He crawls on his journey from here to there,
a small modest part of the whole affair.
Here he comes, there he goes.
Where does he come from?
Nobody knows.
Where is he going?
Nobody knows ---
under my feet, under my toes!

His hundred small feet make the journey slow,
though it looks like he knows where he wants to go.
And when he gets there, what will he do?
What will he eat, centipedes' stew?

He's no bother to me, so what do I care?
No ants in my pants, no stings in the chair!
He's more like a friend in his innocent way
and more to the point, he's here to stay.

When I'm dead and gone, he'll still be down there,
still poking along, still playing his part,
his small humble part
in the whole damned affair.

Kenneth Canatsey lives in Agoura Hills CA with his wife of 33 years. His themes gravitate toward political satire, consequences of the pandemic, and the simple consolations of nature. Allpoetry.com/Kenneth.canatsey

[Patricia Jean Alexander]
A Cornucopia of Blessings

Hear ye; hear ye, come one, come all, listen to my voice, take heed to the call, take a chair of your choice; rest your weary feet. Pull yourself up to the table that is filled with all sorts of salad, a variety of dressings, drinks, fruits, vegetables and meats; even the children are welcomed to come to partake of the Lord's supper that is located in the hall, so brides bring your grooms, there is plenty of food for everyone, and a lot of room, all of the human race can come to enjoy God's grace; so come on over to where the table is spread that is also filled with a variety of bread!

———————————

Grandmapat 2003 lives in Cedar Hill, Texas. I am 72 years old, I like to draw, paint, watch game shows, comedies, and old musicals on television, and I like to play games on my phone. Allpoetry.com/Grandmapat2003

[Dr Fazlul Huq]

Milky White Lilies

Milky white lilies at the mount of a slender stem.
Energized and greeted by void and the green.
Adored by dwellers in land of the dream.
Loved by visitors, kith and kin.

Hypnotized and held in a trance throughout
the day.
That slowly fades only after fireball departs.

Witness them propagate message of peace
and hope.
As they engrave their mark in purest
fragrance.
That engulfs the habitat and furthest
surrounds and repeatedly perturbs silence
of the night.

Let us inhale and energize, stimulate and regenerate.
Let us float in air, glide and dare to achieve the heights.
Let us rejoice and merry but not sadden, mourn or cry.
Let us accept and embrace but not reject and deny.

Mankind and jinn created in best of the mold,
every life has a role to play in Creator's plan.

Don't spend your lifetime in search of shadow.
Don't let whirlwind blow away the parchment.
Don't let your mind and heart suffocate and bleed
and don't live in darkness devoid and deceived.

Love is union, love is power and compassion
is divine.
Hatred is division, hatred is denial and hatred
is a crime.

Milky white lilies at the mount of a slender stem.
Energized and greeted by void and the green.
Adored by dwellers in land of the dream
and loved by visitors, kith and kin.

BScHons;MSc;PhD;DIC;DipEd;MRSC. Pen name Jujube. Over
55000 compositions. Led research on anticancer drugs
Allpoetry.com/Jujube

[Joe Boesch]

The Mirror

Look at yourself in The Mirror and see what you did.
Look at yourself in The Mirror and take control of your id.

Did you mean to do it?
Was it just rage?

Look at yourself in The Mirror and question your place.
Look at yourself in The Mirror and put on a new face.

Do you understand your expression?
Do you understand your mind?

Look at yourself in The Mirror and have a peace of mind.
Look at yourself in The Mirror and stop all the lies.

Do you understand the truth?
Do you understand your mind?

Look at yourself in The Mirror and understand the time.

Do you understand your faith?
Do you understand time?

Look at yourself in The Mirror and get on with life.

Joe Boesch is from Long Island, New York. When not blogging or writing, he roots on the New York Yankees.
Allpoetry.com/Joe_Boesch

[S. Libellule]

Subtle Signs

Nature has her designs
such subtle signs
in the whispery way of things
this deep order that she brings

To elements of each day
how all things pass away
in their own select time
draped loving in rhyme

Until I then pen my final word
know at last I have been heard

Originally from New England, Libellule currently lives outside of
Birmingham, Alabama. Poetic influences include Mary Oliver,
Billy Collins and ee cummings. Allpoetry.com/Little_Dragonfly

[Nathaniel L Shoults]

A Gun Named Callie

A father takes his daughter hunting,
Josh sits with Callie in a boxstand,
The Ant man and Addie come along,
Hoping for another buck to land.

The rain was fallin steady,
Kept the deer sitting still,
The wind whips against the wood,
As they all hope for a kill.

The Ant man especially,
His gun between his feet,
Its rack a new installment,
In the love that is his jeep.

His gun, new as well,
Hasn't achieved its lust for blood,
Never smelled its gun powder,
And watch the deer fall with a thud.

The rain lets up before light,
All the sudden here's a doe,
Then in walks a buck,
Followed by a fellow foe.

They let them little ones pass,
And turned out to be a great choice,
All of a sudden a huge body,
Going from a Pinto to a Rolls-Royce.

Callie now in Ant man's lap,
Only fitting she take the shot,
Big sis got her first 2 weeks ago,
Time for lil sis to tie the knot.

She drops the buck first bullet,
The cherry of the barrel now busted,
They wipe the blood of her first kill,
Across her cheeks, forever encrusted.

First at the club this season,
The deer one not the Fitness of Bally,
Also since she killed first with it,
The guns name is now Callie!

I grew up in the country and have a lot of fond memories. I love putting those memories into poetry. I also like to tell it from their perspective if it's about them. Allpoetry.com/NateDogg5

[Lisa F. Raines]

A Prayer Answered

My dad died a peaceful death
He heard the Latin mass and
Celebrated it with his nurse

I know he asked with
All his belief, all his heart
And all his mind

God, please, I'm yours
In your mercy, in your Oneness
Let me be of your kindness
Please take me home

His clouded eyes
Reached for heaven
And he was gone

AlisRamie is from North Carolina, USA.
Interests include: philosophy, history, international relations,
politics, poetry, art, design, jazz, funk, and some good old soul.
Allpoetry.com/AlisRamie

[Stephen Puls]

Raindrops

Raindrops are like people
There's so many on this earth
Raindrops are like people
Without them there'd be no births
Raindrops are like love and hate
Sometimes they bring a chill
Raindrops are like love and hate
Like love they give a thrill
Raindrops are like life itself
From drop to puddle is fast
Raindrops are like life itself
Like life they do not last
Raindrops are like me and you
Our deaths bring more lives
Raindrops are like me and you
We need them to survive
Stephen ☮ ✌

I am from Boston Massachusetts. Writing is a way of keeping my
soul in balance. I enjoy sitting at a train station early in the
morning. It's peaceful and a great place to collect my thoughts.
Allpoetry.com/Stephen2

[Yvette Louise Melech]

The Lemons Are Coming

I'm in a lemon kinda mood.
One woman, who is a lovely lemon.
I bump into from time to time crossed my path.
On my way back from picking up a pint of milk.
She must have been very beautiful,
when she was once young.
She always looks well groomed.
Yet, she has a hypnotic spell like walk.
If she's a witch, she's a white witch but,
I hope you understand,
I've got nothing against black witches, if they're kind.

Anyhow, once upon a time,
she really pleaded,
I give her our poetry book,
from this magical circle herewith.
" Words With Wings ".
She passed by my door,
asking with deep wants,
of such excitement in her eyes.
I gave her a copy.
Her eyes lit up.

On todays paths crossing between us.
I'd thrown on a copper dress.
Nothing expensive, I found it undoing an old trunk.

She commented on my dress.
Was one of those lucky five-minute wonder things.
I added my father Bog -dan's hat.
That is black, as black, smeared with white dog hairs.
With the addition of lemon paint on my hands.
I'm painting the kitchen ceiling.
I've another few rounds.

I muttered holding my pint of milk.
Chewing one piece of cadburys milk.
Not milk tray.
That chocolate, in that corny advertisement
Where a man jumps off a cliff to give a lady waiting underneath a
chocolate box.
I did so love that ad.
As said, it's so corny.
Like the old Hollywood movies in black and white.
When they're dancing under moonlight.

Anyway, my sweet beautiful friend.
She told me a nail-biting secret from seventeen years ago.
Just as I'd plonked a piece of chocolate in my mouth.
I don't often crave for sweet stuff nowadays,
must be the effect of going lemon.

I was so touched by her confiding.
I offered her my remaining chocolate bar.
She politely declined.
Exclaimed, she'd buy the whole shop of chocolate delight, If she
had only one bite.

I exclaimed, oh, that's rather like X alcoholics.
We smiled.

On waving goodbye,
her two little adorable brown chi-wa-wa's,
went up the river lane rather fast.
I have nightmares about rivers just now.
We have a new "Jack The Ripper ",
catching girls with brown dogs.
Thank goodness mines black.
I doubt he'll head to big cities, but nevertheless,
it sends lemon chilblains up my legs.
I'm watching out more ruthlessly for weirdos.
I do confess.

_____

Yvette Louise Melech is from London UK. Having Scottish and
Polish Parents. She holds a devoted interest in the Art world.
Brought up in the world of art from both parents' work and
interests. Allpoetry.com/Doll_In_The_Cupboard

[Kayla Gradoville]
They Danced

They danced around her while she spilled over at the seams
they danced around her while her lights were agleam
they danced around her while she smiled and seemed pleased
they danced around her while sucking her dreams
they danced around her as she started to scream
they danced around her as her tears streamed
they wept around her as she did plea
they left her as she slipped away never to be seen...
Ever again.

I am Kayla Gradoville, a college graduate preferring to study philosophy and anthropology. A lifelong writer starting in kindergarten where I received my first award for a short story. Allpoetry.com/Schoenbergerk

[Patricia Marie Batteate]

The Night my Life Died

He left in such a rush
The last fight that we had
But this time it was different
He's never been so mad

I knew I hit a nerve
But he had crossed the line
Baring false witness
To my integrity a crime

If I sincerely hurt him
Than there must be some truth
I don't conjure up stories
I find that rather uncouth

The weather was so bad
The sky broke out into tears
I didn't want him flying
He had had too many beers

He was so determined
Almost frantic to get away
I pleaded with him not to go
He insisted he wouldn't stay

I watched his plane disappear
Into the turbulent night
I remember thinking out loud
Did it matter who's wrong or right

I went home all alone
Our place felt so cold
I kept hoping that any moment
His entrance was soon to unfold

The night was so painfully long
Tossing in and out of sleep
Playing back every detail
All I could do is weep

Finally, dawn broke
I felt like I could die
I wanted to reassure him
That I was on his side

I kept trying to reach his phone
But could only get voice mail
So he's playing that game, I thought
Well he can go straight to h—l

I decided to stay home
I needed time to think
My whole being an open nerve
So I sat down and poured a drink

The ringing of the phone
Nearly caught me off guard
I wasn't in the mood to talk
I wished I could just send a card

To my surprise it wasn't him
His sister was on the phone
She said his plane had gone down
Not much more had been known

A tidal wave of emotion
Had crested upon my heart
An upsurge of anxiety
Had torn my whole world apart

Everything had stood still
Time had literally stopped
A free fall from reality
An unexpected drop

The need to always be right
Doesn't matter in the end
When that special someone isn't coming home
What's really left to defend.

I am a 7th generation Californian. I am an engineer, poet and
artist. 'Tolerance is a gauge used to determine just how much a
person is willing to put up with'

Allpoetry.com/Patricia_Batteate

[Lisa F. Raines]

Life's Little Rivulets

Like the Colorado river
Carved the Grand Canyon
Life's passionate rivulets
Etched Mom's every line

Years of happiness and
Disappointments eroded
Her features into soft folds
Marking her long life

We remember her when
She was young and beautiful
And as she got older
We saw her life's experiences

Beauty and wisdom
Earned over her lifetime
Marked her devotion to
God and family

———————

AlisRamie is from North Carolina, USA.
Interests include: philosophy, history, international relations,
politics, poetry, art, design, jazz, funk, and some good old soul.
Allpoetry.com/AlisRamie

[Kristi Weber-Suarez]

Nothing

I've got nothing left to give
No matter how I try
Always tried to keep the peace
But now I wonder why

Why did I do this
And why did I do that
Why did I not end it
When all alone I sat

All those years ago
I should have made that choice
When the voices that live my head
Kept silencing my voice

Voices that I've heard
Since I was just a child
Voices that were spat at me
While she just sat and smiled

Be the little actress
Smile when you are down
I'll give you something to cry about
If you so much as frown

My childhood destroyed
By antiquated views
Every person in my life
It's predestined that I'll lose

So, I grasp it even tighter
Then plunge it in my side
The blood inside comes spilling out
Like all the tears I've cried

Alone I lay there bleeding
In my sorrow I will drown
Because no longer can I hide
And never make a sound

The voices become fainter
As I take my final breath
The nothing will consume
On the other side of death

Born in Ohio and raised in Florida, my sister & mother instilled a love of the spoke word deep in my soul. My family, both past and present, inspire my work. Every word is a piece of my heart. Allpoetry.com/Kristi_Weber

Tender toes buried in sand

Tender toes buried in sand,
I'm on vacation with my girl, my friends, and my band.
The delicate feeling of each and every grain,
Brings butterflies to my stomach and peace to my brain.

Tap dancing butterflies beating,
Was the name of our first song,
It was a cover of a poem, not to be misleading.
We got almost everything, every note wrong.

In the soft moonlight of fiery stars,
We surely found our niche there,
Played outdoor concerts and gigs at the bars,
We had so much fun without worry or care.

Sun-streaked sand kisses,
Would grace my chapped lips,
It was hot, humid, and muggy and time for a dip,
By the ocean, everything was all just a trip.

As a lover of the arts, and a lover of my dearest Scarlet, I treasure
the use of language and visual arts whether descriptive or literal.
Allpoetry.com/Barkdream69

[Michael Defalco]

Chasing Raven

The eye opens.
Thus peers the raven
Black eyes ominously glaze
Overturned now to the torture

Unaware of the ravens heart
I awaken to her love
She waits, sits or sats awakened
To my heart that now unfolds

Only to her poking and prodding
I am alive in my sorry sodden
Soul having drunk you in
I am now satiated

But wait, now your darkness
Compels me to know your very soul
Can it be darker than mine
I would that we were entwined...

———————————

Here is not exciting, fortunate to travel and see the world and
unravel its humanity.

Inching towards septuagenarian externally, internally 22nd full of
hope for life and love. Allpoetry.com/Arcadia

[Steven Gelb]

Cloud Shapes

When I let my mind take flight
I can see airy shapes
In the clouds far above me
Which take me on some wild escapes.
A parade of this fluffy convoy
Reminds me of some shapes in life
A small cloud soon resembles
A tall oak tree so full of strife.

What of this rain cloud scary
With thunder and lightning up above.
Now I see a herd of oxen
Please protect me, God of Love.
I see an anvil cloud advancing
Threating all within its path.
I must escape its evil dealings
And avoid its righteous wrath.

What of more benign illusions
Puffy clouds of purest white
Float along some magic courses
Charging as a skyborne knight.
Moving higher in the reaches
Cirrus clouds may pass review.
They resemble celebrations
Of revelers in an airborne queue.

Clouds, indeed, resemble objects
Taken from our daily lives.
Their shapes depend on the beholder
In this way, their forms arrive.
What to one might be a sky-knight
May to others be a queen.
There is not one true answer.
It depends on what is the scene.

———————

Steven was born in Los Angeles, CA. He enjoys the warm
temperatures and many attractions there. He became interested in
poetry in high school and has continued to feel so to the present
day. Allpoetry.com/Treesky36

[Craig E Hellier]

Morning Refreshes

Dewy mist filters the dawn sun
Aspen leaves, spectrum of color from green to yellow
And orange
Gentle breeze stirs the air
All is new and fresh,
And alive again.

Whitetail deer munch with delight,
The buffet of petunias and marigolds
Planted at the end of the drive
Simply for their pleasure,
Apparently.

Cloud shadows dapple the ground
Placid patterns silently shifting
Grasses and leaves sway
Pleasing to the eye,
And ear.

Just a whiff of morning dew
A hint of the day to come
The wind of new hope
Nudges me forward,

A lone hiker
Intent upon no destination

Moved on by the sunrise
Propelled by possibility.

Today will be better
I'm feeling inspired
Nature's allure
The delicacy of a new start,

Optimistic contentment
Draws my eyes skyward
Soft, billowy clouds
Grace the skies with their elegance,

I wonder what it would be like
To hold one in my hand
The lightweight emptiness
Of something so substantial
But made of nothing.

Under my feet now
The soft carpet of dying photosynthesis
Each step is cushioned
Each step takes me forward,
Onward,
And upward.

Tall trunks sway as the sun warms the hour
Protected in here
Among this umbrella of shade
Along a well-worn track,

My mind is at ease
For the moment, peace,
My soul feels refreshed
In the womb of nature,
Far, far away.

Craig lives in Highlands Ranch, Colorado, and enjoys everything that the great outdoors of the U.S. West has to offer.
Allpoetry.com/Chellier

[Bobbie Breden]

Good Bye, Sweet Angel

Here we are, my sweet Angel
Together at the end of a long road
A road where you and I shared a bit of my life
And I got to share all of yours

You look so tiny and fragile in my lap
Wrapped up In an enormous bath towel
And soon our vet will be here
To tell me what I think I already know

It is time

So while we wait, I cradle you, trying to comfort us both
While I try my best to let you know how much you are loved
And my deep gratitude for your companionship and affection,
Your silliness and unexpected tricks and antics

Like the time when you discovered how to
Change the settings on the television remote
And it took me the better part of a week
To figure out what you'd done

And when I found you on my bathroom counter
Combing your fuzzy face with my favorite hair brush
While you held the brush handle between your paws
I realized I was fortunate that you didn't have thumbs

Ah my pretty little tuxedo diva, you were always your own cat,
Awarding your approval, friendship, and affections only to those
You deemed deserving, while the rest of unworthy humanity
Could just "talk to the paw" as you gave them the cold shoulder

It's been a delightful adventure, my lovely black and white sun
baby
An almost eighteen year long gift, and as many times as I tried
To prepare myself for today, I knew I wouldn't really be ready
Yet here we are, you and I, ready or no, all the same

I watch as your wee paws gently reach for my hand
I stroke your neck and your tiny chin
And bend to softly kiss your head in a final goodbye
As your breathing slows and I watch you leave me

Your brother Baci and I will spend tonight consoling each other
As best we can, with explanations unnecessary, he understands
Tomorrow morning and the rest of this week,
I shall be at loose ends, downsizing bowls, litter boxes, bedding

When I finally find the strength to look at your pictures again
I know I will smile as I remember how much fun we had together
How very grateful I am to have had you and your brothers
As part of my life for even a short while

As I hold you this last time and carry you to the door
To thank you for sharing your life with me doesn't seem enough
Happily, I took the time over the years to tell you "I love you"

But now it is time, and I will miss you, my pretty girl.
Good bye, my sweet Angel.

Retired Lady Leatherneck (US Marine), Renaissance woman, and
a lover of life's mysteries. I'm interested in how others view the
universe, and welcome opportunities to see it through their eyes.
Allpoetry.com/Captain_B2

[Douglas R Colthurst]

Fractured

She wears a fracture
on her face.
She can't see it,
it's been erased.

She was young now,
just defining space.
Violation came by,
gave her no solace.

An event she buried,
but never left that place.
Kind of left a fracture
right on her face.

Adolescence
has many doubts.
It's hard enough to
just fit in.

Where to put the trauma,
perhaps behind the grin?
She was fractured
from this moment on.

You can't confront this.
She can't herself.
For it's not there now.

She can't be fractured.
Oh my God, no no.

It's sad to see what
a mirror can't reflect.
She wears a fracture
on her face.

———————————

Born small town, central Illinois. (350) Educated U. of Illinois, Urbana-Champaign, BS U. of Illinois Dental College DDS. Love writing, painting, cooking, music ,wine, Harley Allpoetry.com/Victortouche

[Stefan Weisenberger]

Senses

This song about
warm coffee on your lips,
ripples of sensations.
The smell of a light roast,
fruity flavors and hint of cinnamon,
the softness of your lips,
the hint of shampoo in your hair
and how it tingles on my face,
the warmth of your body
against mine.
I strum my guitar
strolling through memory
and imagination
looking for you.

World traveller originating in Germany with imprints of North America, Balkans, and the Nordics, in love with Japan and France. Poetry of love, loss, and spirituality. Allpoetry.com/S._O._White

[Drew Cassara]

On A Trip

Illuminating purple night sky,
In morse code
Stars twinkle, h - e - l - l - o.
My identity's detached,
I'm one with the constellations.
Physical perceptions liquidate,
Transcending the imagination.

Questioning my very existence,
2-D iridescent elephants run free
Around a tree in the distance.
Helicopters hover by
And gravitate over a lake,
As combat men fall from ropes
Where tankers await.

From Queens, New York.
I believe in poetry as a form of spontaneity and flow; a stream of consciousness that's summoned from emotion evoked by a peak experience. Allpoetry.com/Cassará

[Deedra Tinsley]

Until The Sun Sets One Final Time

When it seems that life came and passed
Is it because you thought it would surely last
Did you take for granted 'everything' and all around
Then realized you can't retreive anything which was never found
Beauty in our world is for the curious taking
With so much to be discovered or still in the making
If one day you want to live up to your best
Then disregard the lives of all the rest
When the sun shines no more, this just means
You let life pass by with all of its precious scenes

———————————

My siblings, my sons, and my parents have the greatest impact on
my writing . Truly I thank them the most! With love Miss D
Allpoetry.com/Deedra_Tinsley

[Sean Cooke]

Watching

I've sat and watched a man try and change.
It's filled me with both joy and rage.
He was never a man to sit on the side.
He would stick to the centre with unmovable pride.

I've sat and watched this man change.
Age does a lot to alter our perspective.
I find myself questioning your objective?

Here I am asking myself.
What more could I do?
No one can blame others better than you.
After all know that I'm still sitting here.

———————————

I am a 33 year old man from northern England, reading and
writing poetry is now a satisfying and productive part of my life. I
thank my mother and father deeply and all those who read my
poetry. Allpoetry.com/Arsenalfan30

[Leesaan Robertson]

Deepest feelings

Let me express my complete emotions
Give all to him who's vast as earth's oceans
He's handsome and slightly tall
He's my up lifter whenever I fall
If I can't spend my days with him on earth
Tell me what's my life really worth
I'm willing to show him the worst of me
That's how an undying love should be
He's my soul-mate for eternity
Together we can embrace this journey of life
With endless sincerity
I love him from the bottom of my heart
And no-one can break us apart
This love of ours will never perish
He's the man I'll always cherish
In this world, I may never find
Another man like him who's one of a kind
I want to give him my all
But words are not enough to say
I rather show him how I feel in every way.

———————————

I am from St.Ann's bay Jamaica. I am very passionate about writing especially poetry because it speaks to my soul. Allpoetry.com/JamaicanQueen

[Lisa F. Raines]

My Dad died today

Billions of people
Must choose to see
Or not to see
The death all around us

We owe it to the Earth
We owe it to our God
Life's bargain was made
Many millennia ago

Our dust must settle
Buried for an eternity
Waiting for a new world
The next one must be better

Phantom pain streams
From eyes swollen shut
Tragedy should be expected
Accepted, if not understood

———————————

AlisRamie is from North Carolina, USA.
Interests include: philosophy, history, international relations,
politics, poetry, art, design, jazz, funk, and some good old soul.
Allpoetry.com/AlisRamie

[Venugopal K]

A light

To discover myself
I read books in libraries
Listened to religious discourses
They promised heavens

This is groping in darkness
for many years,
Running after invisible mirages
Promising to quench thirst
But seldom delivered.....

Physical laws logically arranged
A lab to experiment,
Teacher well versed ,guides a student
makes him understand the nuances
Of the subject

A great stride in technology
did nothing on psyche
Men is where he is
From beginnings of time since Big Bang

A Big Crunch comes
one finds oneself searching for inner light
while world without illumined
in dazzling lights

I am hydrologist by profession. I am inspired by seeing water to write poetry in this site. Now I am working as professor in civil engineering department in Bharat Institute of technology. Allpoetry.com/Venu_hydrologist

[Hope Lambert]

Permission

It's okay to grieve an "almost" death,
It's not wrong to crave the past.
Two weeks ago you appeared healthy,
A year ago you were well.
Four days ago I almost lost you,
What would I do?
Come find you!
Wrap a scarf around my neck,
Tie it to the highest branch.
It's okay to grieve the past.
It's not wrong to crave death,
When yours becomes real.

––––––––––––

Hope Lambert is originally from San Antonio but currently lives in Edmond, Oklahoma. She writes to ease the burden of the soul. Allpoetry.com/Pretty_Wire

[Andrew Stull]

our old front door

I barely
remember
the sound of
your
voice.

are you the cannon
that fires into
the eye
of a hurricane?

the touch of your
hands and fingers and palms
have grown cold
and long gone.

your kiss?
the disappointment
on your lips and face and eyes
when I'd walk through
our old front door, after coming home
late at night from work.

I could hear you laugh and be happy
until you heard my key jingle
as I opened our old front door.

your sister sat with you
and her happiness died too
when she saw me
walk through
our old front door.

for that, I cannot and will not
blame her.

all three of us
were miserable
in that little home.

misery clouded
the walls behind
our old front door.

being stoned helped me.

I don't know what helped you or her
but I hope you're both happy now
and not miserable.

I'll never forget your kindness
towards the end.

but I'll also never forget
that miserable song you played
on that miserable day
behind our old front door.

I barely
remember
the sound of
your
voice
and
that
makes me
smile.

but I heard that
god damned awful
song today, the one you played
on that miserable day
and it made me
think of
grocery lists
and how
I once
accidentally
bought store brand mayo
and
the
hell that ensued
from doing so.

Andrew Stull is an aspiring novelist and poet from Clarksburg, WV. He uses poetry to help him cope with bipolar disorder. His favorite band is The Killers and has seen them perform live three times. Allpoetry.com/Andrew_Stull

[Kelsey Jean]

Squandered Fairytale

A savage beast you've ripped me wide open,
left bare my most vulnerable and worthy organs.
A once lush and vibrant rainforest
I am now but a puddle - trivial, muddied.
Eyes desperate for glimpse of restoration,
a desert to dry these unrelenting droplets...
pouring down pruning cheeks
now merely a forgotten canvas - waterlogged
by despair and loneliness.
You've dissipated like early morning fog
taking all hope and sanity with you,
packed tight in your suitcase of lies.
I remain - fragmented.
A dazed tenant no longer content
residing in this fleshy abode - a past fortress
of delighted refuge.
Though shattered like breakaway glass
I would relive this nightmare over again...
just to hold you - squandered fairytale - once more.

Kelsey Jean is from Owatonna, Minnesota. For her poetry has often been the most perfect escape. Without poetry, there is no water to replenish or air to breathe - without it there is no life. Allpoetry.com/Kelsey_Jean

[Cory Ford]

Trampled flowers

Unknown are the names of the flowers
That have been trampled
Blood is what makes the grass grow here
Smoke and gun powder is what we breath
And death is our life
You are your only true enemy

My name is Cory Ford and I never fancied myself a poet or the
next Robert Frost, but I do enjoy writing; in fact, I hope to
publish my first book in the next year. Writing has been a dream
of mine. Allpoetry.com/emotears

[Scarlet Ilythia Cope]
asleep not really

looking forward between space never-ending pathetic wave eater
of my brain missing episodes 1-10 fun while it lasted nearly hate
hand one tiny small card broaden door play nearly pointless way
up high stairs regular meals usually a lava eats small amounts of
get your memory back in place I'll stay awaiting that final
statement left in dust in old potato chips

_____

A try at poetry. My name is S.I.C. I do not know what to say at
this point. All I can say is I tried really hard.
Allpoetry.com/PunkRockGirlfriend101

[Lisa F. Raines]

Like skeletons in hollow walls

Some wounds do not heal
They fester under scars
And get buried alive

Unexpected events
Loose these mental tramas
Onto our consciousness

Abandoned memories
Like orphans re-emerging
Are quickly ushered away

Becoming skeletons
Built into hollow walls
Underpinning our fragile psyche

AlisRamie is from North Carolina, USA.
Interests include: philosophy, history, international relations,
politics, poetry, art, design, jazz, funk, and some good old soul.
Allpoetry.com/AlisRamie

[Rachel K. Martin]
The Laughing Crap

He wiped her buttox
felt her lox
on a medeival chair
she sat, oh how it was fair!
he wants to know if you are
he has to think of himself, afar
laughing, at gay
play with her crap, away
it laughs

The poet's name is Rachel K. Martin. She graduated from Saint
Louis University with a B.A. in English and from Webster
University with a M.A. in Patent Agency.
Allpoetry.com/BlueAngel1111

[Steven Gelb]

Forest Green and Azure Blue

"Your favorite colors" you ask me,
Are easy for me to tell,
"The green of the lush forest,
And the azure ocean's swell."
My love for these bright colors,
Is hard to overstate.
They give me such pleasure,
And allow me to create.

How does forest green affect me?
It amazes me without end
With the lushness of the flora
And how naturally it blends.
From the towering trees above me
To the smallest plant below
The greenish vegetation
Delights the whole meadow.

What of the bluish colors,
That are alluring to my eye,
The deep blue of the ocean
Or the azure of the sky?
Forget not the blue gemstones
That shimmer as they shine,
The topaz or the turquoise
Are simply so divine.

Forest green and azure blue
Strike in me a chord
They both are very thrilling,
And make my spirits soar.
Besides the green of trees or plants
Or blue of sea or sky
These colors are my favorites
And lift me, oh so, high.

Steven was born in Los Angeles, CA. He enjoys the warm
temperatures and many attractions there. He became interested in
poetry in high school and has continued to feel so to the present
day. Allpoetry.com/Treesky36

[S. Libellule]

Primary Colors

This very choice
so reflects Her voice
with colors subtly chosen
to paint a masterpiece

Cerulean blue
evergreen hue
frosted white
all mixed just right

To dapple the snow
with a resonant glow
snatching my breath
before I can take it

What a sacred blend
from beginning to end
upon the tender canvas
of this humbled life

Leaving me here
to only revere
with nothing left

but to write

Originally from New England, Libellule currently lives outside of Birmingham, Alabama. Poetic influences include Mary Oliver, Billy Collins and ee cummings. Allpoetry.com/Little_Dragonfly

[Andreas Pfluger]

And finally we bloom

At first we`re deeply buried in the earth
seed of potential, ready to take birth
Alone, caged, unconscious in the dark
Missing just that final spark

Unknowing of what and why we are
Alone, afraid, unaware, yet avatar
Boundless, marvelous human creature
Limitless, unconfined by its very nature

Suddenly there`s some major shift within
Nothing like it`s always been
Kundalini Shakti`s gentle touch
An urge to change, almost too much

An impulse drives one to break out
This must be what it`s all about
Life itself brings one to grow
Surrendering to natural flow

Abruptly there is all this light
A new world wonderful and bright
All around are all these others
We welcome you, Sisters and brothers

All unique yet all the same
Entirely animated by Life's flame
Driven to grow and to expand
Wonders and miracles beforehand

Each day a gift, we learn, and we explore
Life beautifully resonates with our core
Teachings gained out of interactions
Served to us in little fractions

We grow older, we grow stronger
Meanwhile our stems get longer
One day we might develop a leaning
To ask for purpose, ask for meaning

Finding this answer seems impossible a task
Who might help us, who might we ask?
While still wondering we might flower
Without a thought standing in our power

Could after all this be the key?
Just learn, bloom, flower, simply be?
Not living life but let Life live us?
Maybe I try going through life thus

I firmly believe that it's our responsibility as a human family to
find a way back to living in accordance with Gaia and trust that
"nature knows the way". Namasté
Allpoetry.com/Livefromtheheart

[Lisa F. Raines]

blank verse - a haiku

no more happy rhymes
the poem doesn't end, but
moments fade away

AlisRamie is from North Carolina, USA.
Interests include: philosophy, history, international relations,
politics, poetry, art, design, jazz, funk, and some good old soul.
Allpoetry.com/AlisRamie

[Anne Harbron]

Raining Sunshine

The sun is shining, or is it raining?
The birds are humming, or are they singing?
The clouds are sleeping, or are they resting?
Forming beautiful images to keep us thinking.

The bees are busy searching for flowers.
They can fly for hours and hours.
The world never stops, and has so many powers.
Whether it's raining or sunshine.

The moles are digging to find adventure.
Or maybe just going to a lecture?
Even the grass is growing and going somewhere.
Whether it's raining or sunshine.

When you are asleep, the world is awake
Moving and slithering are the snakes.
The mosquitoes are waiting for fresh blood.
And the trees are growing new leaf buds.

The world and its powers are so mystical.
Even though some beings are hypocritical.
Maybe also too political?
Whether it's raining or sunshine.

Everyday it's raining beautiful sunshine.
Everyday it's a beautiful sunrise.
This is the time to rise.
And feel the love from our skies.

Artist, Painter and Designer of Quirky Art. Poetry is my way to express how I feel and a way for me to help others. Words can make a diffence between a smile and a frown. Laughing or crying. Allpoetry.com/skyla1234

[Courtney Martin]

Illumination

Twilight
pierces the sky,
dismantling darkness.
And as persuasive as she is
she's made me open my eyelids again.
The sky's her canvas, day and night,
shadows dance, until
we meet anew,
twilight.

I live in central Alabama. I enjoy writing both poetry and lyrics, and in my spare time I like to play video games and make art. Allpoetry.com/C.Martin

[Melissa Louise Davis]
Broken

She's strong on the outside, but on the inside she's crying
Dying to break free from the shackles that bind her
The pain that blinds her
Haunted by a multitude of dark moments
Love was conditional, she was never enough
The world is tough
Consequences cut
Opportunities were missed
Kissed herself goodbye
She had no "Catcher in the Rye"
She fell and fell hard
Her heart has been barred
What is love?
Cheated by the years of perversion
She never knew
And when she thought she did
They annihilated any sliver of hope

Melissa Louise is a freelance artist and writer who currently resides in North Texas. Her work deeply reflects her experiences and emotions. Allpoetry.com/MelissaLouise

[Kentrell Parker]

How Nature punished the body

Nature has a way of punishing the body,
if it's not well cared for.
The punishment is to the flesh but
an inconvenience to the dweller
within the flesh.
The body complains of pain and suffering,
as the dweller,
reflecting Itself as
high projects,
great purposes, and
noble inspirations.
As the body becomes ill,
Nature demolished it back to dust,
another imperfect reflection.

Kentrell Parker is a Poetess from Pahokee, Fla. I've always had a
passion to write but never took it seriously, until 10 years later. I
found my niche in writing Poetry and the rest was history.
Allpoetry.com/Theartwithinyo

[Paul Crocker]

Decomposing Of An Apple

You came to me with that fruit in your hand.
The ripest of the tree.
Such love and happiness you had planned.
But time has declared it not to be.

Your intentions were pure and true.
For the sphere of nature's giving.
Vividly you remember its blushed rosy hue.
Before it gave up on living.

The oldness shows with the wrinkles indent.
Its skin is not so firm.
The juice has soured, unable to pay the rent.
A prime opportunity for the invasive worm.

Age spots cover it like a blanket of dread.
Such an awful existence to grapple.
The youthful orb is now decayed and dead.
This is the decomposing of an apple.

————————

I am a poet from Bristol, UK. I started writing poems in 2001. I
enjoy both reading and writing poetry and everything connected
with it. Allpoetry.com/PoeticXscape

[Rachel E Robb]

Motivation in the Wild

A snake in the midst of its chaos

Calculating

Wearing a skin of warm and inviting colors
Which effectively veils the poison beneath the surface

Circling slowly

Calculating

Looking for an open shot
A place to puncture the skin

Driven Forward by fear
Not hate

For protection
Not revenge

Calculating the risk
There is no reward

Except Survival

So I've always loved words. They help me define myself and
challenge others. Words help me choose the people who are
closest to me. Allpoetry.com/Rachelegregs

[Andrew lee Joyner]

Words that cut deep

The sound of silence,
the hatred of violence

A way of peace, a life of zen
Treading close to a hellish sin

How it happened, one cannot say
It will change, hopefully someday

More to tell, out of hell
lack of health, not very well
before I die, to life's dismay
"Words can hurt, every single day"

I started writing poetry at a young age, it became a hobby of mine
and now it's my life, I love to read and write. My inspiration is
life, my sister is my muse Allpoetry.com/Andrew_Lee

[Leah X]

My warm velvet shame

For the last time
I will keep it stored away
And it will go with me
It will probably be the same
I hope for someone else
To turn and come forward
For in order to understand it all
One should explain complexities

As she enters
This is the warm velvet box
This is the place that keeps all the secrets
Tell her, she's the doctor
She can handle the shocks

This is the warm velvet box
Soft and disgustful, but i no longer long for her
Dreaming of the tenderness
The tremble in the hips upon entry
As if she were kissing Mary's lips
Just at that point
Before the turning away
There is a silent panic

"What are you doing here?"
"Get out bitch"

Hearing the echo's before the conscious does
And then they all join in the turning away
From what they don't understand
Fear, dispel, anguish, antagonises about having nothing
Light is turning to shadow
She can feel their faces turn, hide, turn in
Total abandonment
"You're on your own now."

Poetry is my friend and my enemy. It allowed me to speak
without anyone listening. However the cost has been huge.
Allpoetry.com/Jeda_04

[Gary Adcock]

Today I climbed a mountain

today I climbed a mountain just to gaze below
soaking up nature's beauty in the sun's warm glow
like a painting on a canvas, colors explode everywhere
looking down upon these wonders calmness fills the air

today I climbed a mountain to escape a world of hate
pondering all life's questions, often fearing for our fate
ashamed of man's behavior, I pause for self reflection
prayers softly spoken, seeking guidance and direction

today I climbed a mountain so my spirit might enjoy
the beauty life has to offer; a world man cannot destroy
many lessons we can learn just by looking to our past
we must take care of one another if love is meant to last

tomorrow I'll leave this mountain, my work now begins
searching for the answer to man's temptation and sins
if we can be like nature, letting shades of beauty show
tranquility can be found, peaceful winds again will blow

––––––––––––––––––

Growing up in the Flint hills of Kansas I have always been a
dreamer. I love the outdoors and good music. When you combine
the two you have the makings of a great day!
Allpoetry.com/Gary_Adcock

[Kristi Weber-Suarez]

Queen of the Damned

Believe them if you will
And hate me if you must
But know that you are the one
Who broke every bit of trust

You threw me to the street
And let your engine roar
You ran me over once then twice
And left me bleeding on the floor

But death and hell don't want me
The fucking devil turned and fled
As once more I rose defiant
Standing in the puddle where I bled

But just remember I hate myself
More than you could ever hated me
And I punish myself everyday
In ways you'll never see

So, live your life with all the love
And I wish you all that's good
And just know that I have loved you
With everything I could

I won't interfere,
In your life, In any way
Cause I've always loved you far too much
To force myself to stay

The tears I've cried are liquid fire
They've burned into my soul
The years of hell that I've endured
Will force me toward this goal

So here is my final wish for you
Take it for what it's worth
Live your life & miss me not
When I leave this earth.

Don't cry in my coffin
Just dance upon my grave
Cause I'm already the queen of hell
I gave up being saved.

Born in Ohio and raised in Florida, my sister & mother instilled a love of the spoke word deep in my soul.
Allpoetry.com/Kristi_Weber

[Lisa F. Raines]

Your Little Hand

Roll up the sky and
Blow out the moon
No more wishes on
The first star tonight

You held our little hands
And taught us to pray
I held your little hand
And learned about forgiveness

May you know our love
Is with you, as
We know you will
Always be a part of us

We miss you, Mom

AlisRamie is from North Carolina, USA.
Interests include: philosophy, history, international relations,
politics, poetry, art, design, jazz, funk, and some good old soul.
Allpoetry.com/AlisRamie

[Robert Poleski]

Changes II - Time

alive- never the same
bloom- languish
then bloom again
the lotus flower forsaken in the mud
sleeps at night
awakes with the sun
resilient
rises from wilt what feels like
dying

constant changes
surpassing feats had done before
learning twilights
drifting in time warps
not ever the same-
like a mountain river
a river of time
time you cannot touch still
the wind in ears
air breathed
with memories of deeds done before
changing the perspective--
experience prevails
awaken and conscious
of changes

what remains- acceptance
so not to be haunted by memories
healing
be ready for new beginnings
tides rising and falling
"the sun also rises
and the sun goes down"
embrace the light
accept the darkness
in darkness
restart the twilight

love
brings the salvation back
the pain of loneliness connects to a healing world
and the healing starts
when redemption comes
torturers become the remedy
a constant change
renewed start
hominid becomes a new
improved god--

Human

_____

What I see is my own world, my whole intimate universe, with
my mind, my heart, looking inside things, inside feelings, what
makes it laugh or cry, love or hate, what makes it feel pleasure or
pain. Allpoetry.com/Robert_Poleski

[Nathaniel L Shoults]

The First Wall Hanger

Being the first to do anything,
Is always a great one upper,
Something to hold over your siblings,
Like calling shotgun, or finishing supper.

In a family where dad is a hunter,
Three girls wait on the wings,
The eldest of the bunch,
Hopes a big one the day brings.

Addie sits with her dad,
She's excited but vigilant,
Dad has the heater going for her,
So she doesn't get whiny and petulant.

Her comfort level maxed,
Heater blasting, phone in hand,
Dad is removing clothes,
Feeling like he's in a desert land.

The sun starts going down now,
Its getting harder and harder to see,
Then they spot movement on the hill,
Raise the scope, what could it be.

A massive silhouette with horns,
Sits in the scope's center piece,
"Addie get your butt in gear,
You're gonna take down this beast".

As she aims down the sight,
He helps hold the gun rock steady,
She's aimed at his shoulder,
And is willing and ready.

She pulls slowly on the trigger,
But here's a click instead,
What the heck has happened?
Why is the deer not dead?

In all the excitement,
The safety never got switched to fire,
But was then quickly flipped,
Like a professional murder for hire.

Shot to the throat,
The buck collapses straight down,
Blood pouring from the wound,
While it falls to the ground.

Her first buck in the books,
It is a wall hanger as well,
Looks great in the house,
But somebody doesn't like the smell!

I grew up in the country and have a lot of fond memories. I love putting those memories into poetry. I also like to tell it from their perspective if its about them. Allpoetry.com/NateDogg5

[Lisa F. Raines]

It's me

I so looked forward to
Your Christmas cards
Pictures of your daughter
She looked so much like you

How old is she now
When your Dad died
You stopped writing
Christmases aren't the same

Why didn't I write
Or keep your address
I've searched for years
To tell you I love you

I miss you
It's me

AlisRamie is from North Carolina, USA.
Interests include: philosophy, history, international relations,
politics, poetry, art, design, jazz, funk, and some good old soul.
Allpoetry.com/AlisRamie

Made in the USA
Columbia, SC
25 April 2023

15726742R00122